—— **THE ESSENTIAL** ——

FIRST-TIME HOME BUYER'S BOOK

An Insider's Guide on How to Buy a House,
Get a Mortgage, and Close a Real Estate Deal—
Without Losing Your Mind

BY THE EDITORS AT

realtor.com®

Book cover design by Teri Joe

Book cover photograph © living4media/Bjarni B. Jacobsen

Photos of the homes in Chapter 7 are courtesy of iStock and the following photographers: Marje (bungalow), jhorrocks (Cape Cod), lillisphotography (Colonial), cirano83 (French country), Greg Chow (mid-century modern), RyPle (ranch), csfotoimages (Spanish), EricVega (townhouses), quackersnaps (Tudor), ksmith0808 (Victorian).

Acknowledgments: We are indebted to the many writers who have contributed to this book: Liz Alterman, Daniel Bortz, Angela Colley, Maureen Dempsey, Cathie Ericson, Audrey Ference, Margaret Heidenry, Jamie Wiebe, and others.

ISBN: 978-1-54396-571-1

Table of Contents

Introduction

Are You Ready to Buy a Home?

"There's no place like home."

—*The Wizard of Oz*

If you're looking at this book, you're probably hoping to buy a home—perhaps your first. Or maybe you *have* purchased property before, but were overwhelmed by the process and want more guidance this time around. In either case, you've come to the right place!

Let's face it—buying a house is a life-changer. Do it right, and you've scored a sweet retreat from the world's uncertainties. Pick the *wrong* place, however, and it could land you in a money pit or a neighborhood you hate, where you will be stuck for awhile (homes don't come with refund policies).

Bottom line? Buying a home is not an impulse purchase, but one that should be pondered carefully. To test just how prepared you are, ask yourself these five questions to see where you stand.

Question #1. Can you afford a home?

The first step is to find out whether you *can* buy a house, given your current financial situation. Is your income high enough? Are your debts and other expenses under control? If you want some help with the number-crunching, plug your income and expenses into an online home affordability calculator to get a sense of whether you can afford a home and how much money you should spend.

Question #2. Does it make sense to buy rather than rent?

The whole "Rent or buy?" question depends on which housing market you're in, because prices and inventory can make a huge difference. The good news is that an online rent vs. buy calculator can crunch the numbers for you. You'll enter the rent you're currently paying (or are able to pay) and the ZIP code you want to live in. What you'll get: a comparison of the cost of buying a home, versus renting in that area.

POP QUIZ

How old are first-time home buyers?

According to the National Association of Realtors® Profile of Home Buyers and Sellers, the median age of first-time home buyers is 32.

Question #3. Are you planning to stay put for a while?

Generally, the longer you're going to be living in a home, the smarter it is to buy rather than rent. As a rule of thumb, home buyers should plan to stay put for at least five years. If you already know that you are likely to move in that time frame, you may have your answer: Stick with renting.

Question #4. Are your retirement savings on track?

We know, we know: Retirement seems a long way off. Still, it's crucial to start storing those nuts early. So if you're neglecting your 401(k) to funnel all your funds toward a home purchase, that may not be the best allocation of resources (particularly if your employer matches funds, which is free money).

Another reason: Setting aside money in a retirement account must be done the year you earn that income; you can't go back later with a wad of cash and hope to squeeze it in.

Here's some good news: Much of the money you put into a retirement account like an IRA can be withdrawn for a first-time home purchase, provided you meet certain requirements.

When in doubt on what to do, consult a financial adviser who can help you strike a balance between saving for a house *and* your future.

Question #5. Are you ready for the responsibility?

With a rental, you can just call your landlord to fix that leaky faucet. With a home you own, it's all on you. So ask yourself if you're willing to forgo weekend bar crawls with friends in order to mow the lawn or patch the roof.

All that said, there are low-maintenance homes you can own: Condos, for instance, require less upkeep, because you pay for others to take care of these tasks. Still, by and large, homeownership comes with responsibilities, so you should be sure you're ready to embrace these obligations with open arms.

POP QUIZ

Do people hold off on buying a home until they're hitched?

Not always! Here's a breakdown of the relationship status of home buyers:

- 63% are married couples
- 18% are single females
- 9% are single males
- 8% are unmarried couples

Ready to buy a home? How this book can help

If you answered "yes" to most of the questions above, then you may truly be ready to buy a home—and that's where this book comes in.

Whether you're a first-time home buyer or a repeat customer who could stand to brush up on a few skills, there's a steep learning curve when you're navigating today's marketplace. And few know this better than we do!

Realtor.com offers an extensive inventory of real estate listings. Every day, millions flock to us not only to peruse beautiful pictures of homes, but also for much-needed advice on how to purchase a place of their own. By interviewing top experts in the real estate field—financial planners, mortgage lenders, real estate agents, brokers, and others—we help guide home buyers through their journey, making sure they find the best house, at the best price, with a great mortgage, and more.

In this book, we won't barrage you with a slew of statistics or obscure terms. We firmly believe that even the most complex aspects of real estate can be explained in plain old English. Our aim is to keep you feeling confident throughout the home-buying process that you're asking the right questions, making the right decisions, and ultimately choosing the very best home for you.

So whether your version of the American Dream includes a sprawling Mediterranean mansion, a midcentury modern apartment, or a quaint Craftsman bungalow on a small patch of grass you can call your own, read on. With the right planning and prep work, it's all within reach. Good luck!

Sincerely,

Judy Dutton, Editor

Chapter 1

The Top 10 Benefits of Buying a Home

"Real estate cannot be lost or stolen, nor can it be carried away. Purchased with common sense, paid for in full, and managed with reasonable care, it is about the safest investment in the world."

—President Franklin D. Roosevelt

Buying a home may be the American dream, but it's also a monumental task: You have to clean up your credit, apply for a mortgage, visit tons of houses, scrape together a down payment, and then move all your worldly possessions after you close the deal. Phew!

So then why do millions of Americans go through the trouble? Because they know that whatever hassles they must endure are far outweighed by the benefits of buying a home.

If you need some inspiration to start house hunting or just want to make sure you're taking advantage of all that homeownership has to offer, check out this list of the top 10 perks that will repay your hard work from now well into retirement.

Benefit #1. Predictable monthly housing payments

Usually, a landlord can raise your rent whenever a lease expires—and sometimes by as much as he pleases. But as a homeowner, if you get a mortgage with a fixed interest rate, you can lock in a predictable mortgage payment for as long as 30 years.

As such, instead of worrying about fluctuating rents, "Homeowners can create a budget knowing that their principal and interest payments won't rise ... ever," says Brian Davis, a real estate blogger at SparkRental.com.

Bonus: Your housing budget goes toward your homeownership, not your landlord's.

Benefit #2. It's often cheaper to own than rent

Sure, there are upfront costs of buying a house, like that massive down payment. However, "After that, the monthly outlay of owning a home is much less than paying rent in many markets in the U.S.," says Davis.

(To figure out if buying is the more affordable choice in your area, check out an online rent vs. buy calculator).

Benefit #3. A great financial investment

"Owning a house provides you with a valuable asset and financial stability," says Peter Vekselman, a real estate professional with Yates Estates Keller Williams in Georgia.

While a home's value may rise or fall based on factors such as where it's located and how the economy is doing, you can generally expect real estate to appreciate by 3% to 4% per year, driven by inflation and natural population growth. Stocks may rise faster—or drop. So by comparison, real estate is a relatively safe investment. Plus a house has one noteworthy bonus that stocks can't lay claim to: It provides a roof over your head!

Benefit #4. Tax benefits

Homeownership can come with tax benefits, and while the Tax Cuts and Jobs Act passed in 2017 changed the rules somewhat, there's still a lot to consider. One of the biggies continues to be the ability to deduct the interest on a mortgage up to $750,000. (Folks whose mortgages kicked in before December 15, 2017, can deduct the interest on up to a $1 million loan). Even though the rules have changed recently, what you can count on is that mortgages that have recently been taken out will yield greater tax savings.

"The way mortgage payments are amortized, the first ones are almost all interest," says Wendy Connick, owner of Connick Financial Solutions in Crescent City, CA. (See how your loan amortizes and how much you're paying in interest with an online mortgage calculator.)

You can also deduct private mortgage insurance and the interest on a home equity line of credit (provided the money is used specifically to buy, build, or improve your property). There are other tax breaks, depending on your circumstances, so be sure to take advantage of all that apply. Because, as Liane Jamason, a broker associate with Florida's Jamason Realty Group, explains, "This allows you to keep more of your hard-earned money."

Benefit #5. Freedom to make modifications

What renter hasn't thought, "I'd really love to paint/alter/knock down this wall to..."? But, of course, you can't—not without the landlord's blessing. And even if you are allowed to renovate your rental, it's the landlord who will ultimately benefit. (Especially if you do a really awesome job at it.)

Homeowners, on the other hand, typically don't need permission. They can paint any room any color, replace the cabinets, retrofit their living room as a detailed replica of the Millennium Falcon, or make pretty much any other modifications they wish. While government building codes and homeowners associations (HOAs) place some restrictions on what you can do (particularly to a home's exterior), there's generally just a lot more leeway when you own. You can live by your own home decor rules, whatever they may be.

Benefit #6. More privacy

Houses—particularly those made of concrete and stucco—provide a greater sound barrier and more privacy from your neighbors than many rental apartments. Plus, "When you own, you can also make your own modifications, such as putting up a fence for added privacy," says Jamason.

Benefit #7. A built-in rainy day fund

Homeownership provides you with the opportunity to borrow money on the equity you will build up by consistently paying your mortgage. Securing a home equity loan at a relatively low interest rate "will enable you to get financing for an emergency, large project, or other expense," says Vekselman.

Benefit #8. Community ties

Owning a house you plan to stay in for a while also allows you to have an impact on your community, since your taxes will benefit local infrastructure, schools, and organizations.

Benefit #9. A secure retirement

A home can be the ultimate nest egg, providing you with a great investment for retirement. The longer you own a house, the more it should eventually be worth.

As you get older, you can sell the home and use the proceeds to purchase or rent something smaller. Another option: Rent out your house while you travel, to offset the costs of your post-retirement globetrotting.

Benefit #10. It's yours!

This may seem fairly obvious, but it's worth emphasizing: With a rental, you run the risk of getting kicked out at the end of your lease (and sometimes earlier). With a home, you can live there indefinitely. And isn't it comforting to know you'll always have a roof over your head?

Chapter 2

Your First-Time Home Buyer Checklist

"Don't wait to buy real estate, buy real estate and wait."

—Will Rogers, actor

As everyone knows, you can't just waltz into a house and declare, "I'll take it!" Long before you get to making that offer and even before going to your first open house, there are a ton of things to do and to prepare.

Worried you might forget something? Here's a checklist of everything you need to do to get ready to buy a home. We'll delve into all of these topics in greater depth later in these pages, but feel free to refer back to this list to see where you are in the process.

☑ Check your credit score

Do not start browsing homes until you have checked your credit score. This is the number that mortgage lenders will look at to determine whether you are "creditworthy," and thus dictates whether you'll qualify for a home loan, and the rates you will get. The higher your credit score, the lower your interest rate—and that's what you're going for.

The first step is to shop for a house

We know that checking out houses is the fun part ... but stop right there. Even if you think you're just browsing, you run the risk of setting your heart on a property that's priced higher than what you can afford. To avoid dashed hopes, make sure your finances and credit score are in top-notch shape first.

☑ Clean up any credit blemishes you can

Any surprises on that credit report? Credit errors are more common than you might think, so contact the credit bureau to correct any erroneous information. Got credit that's less than stellar? Chapter 4 of this book will help you get it in shape.

☑ Figure out how much home you can afford

Next, make sure you are clear about how much home you can afford. An online home affordability calculator can help you determine your monthly mortgage payment, adjusting for variables such as the size of your down payment, your mortgage type, and current interest rates. You can also get an official estimate by following our next tip...

☑ Shop for a mortgage lender

"A prospective home buyer should make one of their earliest stops with a mortgage originator, to see if they can qualify for a mortgage and confirm how much of a mortgage they can afford," says real estate agent Steve

Ujvagi with Keller Williams Realty Atlanta Partners. Different mortgage shops offer a wide variety of rates and programs, so shop around to find the best rate and mortgage option for you.

☑ Secure mortgage pre-approval

Once you've found the mortgage that's right for you, you'll want to show sellers that you have what it takes to buy their home. In hot markets, mortgage pre-approval is almost required for a seller to take your offer seriously. That's because it spells out exactly how much a lender has agreed to loan you, thus assuring the seller that you're both willing *and* able.

☑ Save up for a down payment

To get the best interest rates and lowest fees, you'll ideally want to make a 20% down payment on a home. That's a lot of money! If that amount is out of reach, don't worry—many people put down less, but it's still a big chunk of change, so start squirreling away those nuts now.

☑ Sit tight!

Once you're ramping up to buy a home, it's wise to not make any—we repeat, *any*—major changes in your life or, most important, your finances.

"Do not switch jobs. Do not buy a new car. Do not even buy furniture or apply for a new credit card, which could affect your credit," says Ujvagi. "Just a credit pull alone from a car dealership or a furniture store is enough to affect your credit score and could cause you to lose a home."

☑ Find a real estate agent

There's no reason to go it alone—having an agent helping you can make the whole process much easier.

"In times like these, with a limited number of homes on the market, a buyer needs a great real estate agent to make sure they find their dream home," says Ujvagi.

Don't just take the first real estate agent referred to you by friends or family. Instead, use online tools like realtor.com's Find a Realtor database, where you can pinpoint a professional with a proven track record who specializes in your desired neighborhood and price range.

Your down payment must be 20%

Sure, a 20% down payment is ideal if you want the best interest rates and lowest fees. But many lenders will be glad to offer up home loans with 10% or 5% down, or even as little as 0%, based on your circumstances. Plus, over 2,000 down payment assistance programs across the country are willing to help, saving home buyers an average of $5,965 upfront (provided applicants meet eligibility requirements in terms of income, occupation, or credit). Many home buyers miss out on this financial assistance because they aren't aware of these programs, or assume they don't qualify. Don't be one of them!

☑ Make a wish list

Of course, this list may be a very long one, but you need to be realistic about what elements are truly "wishes" and which ones are nonnegotiable needs—such as number of bedrooms, a fenced yard for a pet, a specific school district, walking distance to the bus stop, etc. Sometimes it's helpful to divide your list into three categories: must-have elements, followed by items that would be nice to have (e.g., a bonus room or home office) and your dream features (e.g., in-ground swimming pool).

☑ Browse listings online

Check out online real estate listings (on sites like realtor.com) to start to figure out what properties are available in your area. Search by price, number of bedrooms, location, and other variables to start narrowing down your options.

☑ Visit open houses

Poring over online listings is one thing; seeing the properties in person is quite another. Take advantage of open houses as a low-stress way to visit several homes in one day. Map your strategy in advance, and while you're in each home, take photos and notes, so they don't all run together in your mind.

☑ Check out the neighborhood

You've undoubtedly heard the adage "Location, location, location." What that essentially means is that you're not just buying the property you're looking at; you're also buying into the whole neighborhood. That's why you have to be certain that it has the vibe and amenities you want. Savvy home buyers know that the best way to find out more about the area is to meet the neighbors and then visit at various times of the day and night to see what it's really like.

Lessons from listings

What are some specific features that make a neighborhood hot? Based on our analysis of realtor.com listing data, here's a snapshot of how quickly certain local amenities help sell a home, and for how much:

🔥🔥 **Hottest Location** 🔥
Median number of days on market and list price

Winner Good school: **76** days
$330,000

Stadium: **77** days
$250,000

Shopping: **79** days
$217,000

Transportation: **88** days
$280,000

Hospital: **95** days
$192,000

Data: realtor.com® / Image: iStock (bluebearry, Askold Romanov, IconicBestiary, Meilun, Andrej Ivosev)   realtor.com graphic

Chapter 3

How to Save Money for a House

> Lucy: I know how you feel about all this Christmas business, getting depressed and all that. It happens to me every year. I never get what I really want. I always get a lot of stupid toys or a bicycle or clothes or something like that.
>
> Charlie: What is it you want?
>
> Lucy: Real estate.
>
> —*A Charlie Brown Christmas*

When you're wondering how to save money for a house, it can start to feel as if you'll never scrape together enough for a down payment.

Yeah, you already know that Rome wasn't built in a day. Well, the same holds true for building a down payment. It takes time!

Still, as long as you grease the gears early (like *now*), you'll barely notice you're saving until—boom!—one day in the foreseeable future, you'll be sitting on a pile of money that could pave the way to homeownership.

Sound good? Good. Here's how to get started.

Trim those unnecessary expenses

OK, let's shift those preconceived notions. Contrary to popular belief, the answer to how to save money for a house *isn't* mostly about grueling sacrifice—like holing up in your apartment under a bare light bulb, eating ramen, and piggybacking off your neighbors' Wi-Fi.

"It's about a lifestyle change," says Travis Sickle, a financial adviser with Sickle Hunter Financial Advisors in Tampa, FL. A more sustainable strategy, he says, is to pinpoint your silent money siphons. Odds are, you could try some of the following cost-cutting measures without feeling the pinch:

- Replace your $250 monthly cable service with a $10 Netflix standard streaming account, and you'll save $2,880 per year.

- Cut that languishing gym membership—at $50 per month, you'd save $600 a year. Go running instead!

- Packing lunch will save you about $60 a month—or $720 a year.

- Bike to work. For a 10-mile commute, biking can save you around $5 a day, according to Kiplinger—or $1,250 a year.

- Start a coin jar. Saving all your loose change can have a big impact— up to $700, according to financial blogger J.D. Roth.

- As a general rule, turning down your thermostat just three degrees full-time could shave almost 10% off your electrical bill, netting you $20 a month on a $200 bill, or $240 a year. Of course, this will vary by area and whether you need heat year-round, but consider it no-brainer savings to snuggle up at home in a sweater.

- Curb those dinners and drinks out at restaurants, which can quickly add up. If you typically shell out $40 three times a week, reduce that to one evening a week, and you'll save $80—or $4,160 per year. (Bonus: It'll make those times you *do* indulge more special!)

And if you and your significant other team up and try all of the above, that would amount to $10,550 per person, or $21,100 in only one year. Just remember that when you're thinking of ordering a third glass of artisanal craft beer.

POP QUIZ

Is buying a home a good investment?

A full 84% of people polled by the National Association of Realtors think buying a home is a good investment that can help secure your financial future.

Open a dedicated account

If you don't have a savings account, now's the time to open one. A checking account is great for daily expenses, but when it comes to saving money—well, they don't call them *savings* accounts for nothing. You'll earn interest on your balance, plus there's a lot to be said for the mental benefit of having a specific place to stash your down payment. While interest rates haven't been very impressive in recent years, it's still great to have a dedicated account where you can see how you're progressing toward your goal.

As an alternative, CDs and money market accounts offer higher gains than savings. You'll need a larger minimum balance than for a regular savings account, but your goal is to make it grow, not shrink, right? If you're using a CD, just make sure you don't withdraw the money before the time is up, or you'll face some stiff penalties.

POP QUIZ

How many home buyers struggle with a down payment?

According to NAR, 13% of home buyers polled said that saving for a down payment was the most difficult step of the home-buying process. As for what was holding them back, 50% blamed college loans, 37% credit card debt, and 35% car loans.

Automate your savings

If you're struggling to put enough money away because of the constant temptation to blow your paycheck, consider automating the process. Ask your employer if you can have your paycheck deposited into multiple accounts—if so, instruct it to send a certain percentage of your salary directly into your savings account. Or go through your bank, setting up automatic withdrawals from your checking to a savings account that will force you to keep your spending in check.

Tap into your IRA

An IRA, in addition to being a tax-friendly retirement vehicle, allows you to withdraw up to $10,000 for a home. Just be careful with this method, as you will be denting your retirement funds. But combined with other savings, it can quickly add some heft to your growing nest egg.

Check out down payment assistance programs

Depending on the city and state you live in, you may be eligible for down payment assistance programs, which provide money to help people buy a home. Most offer up to $15,000, typically in the form of a grant or low-interest loan, and require that your income be lower than the area's median. But even if you make more, do your research—there are programs that provide funds for higher-income households.

If saving up for a down payment is a challenge for you, it may surprise you to know that you don't always need to save 20% for a down payment. With certain kinds of loans, you can get away with a down payment as low as 3.5% (for Federal Housing Administration, or FHA, loans) or even 0% (U.S. Department of Agriculture, or USDA, loans).

Can mom and dad pitch in on the down payment?

You bet! Many first-time home buyers get financial help from their parents to make the down payment. Just keep in mind that the money they give should be a gift—i.e., with no obligation to pay your parents back. The reason: If a lender suspects that the money might be a loan, repaying said loan will be factored into your mortgage approval amount, and you'll qualify for less than you might have wanted.

In order to *prove* it's a gift, you may need to provide your lender a signed letter stating that the money is indeed a gift, not a loan that must be repaid at a later date. Different lenders have slightly different rules on what they require, so be sure to check with them first.

There's also a limit to how much someone can gift you—tax-free, at least. Under the current rules, each person giving can give up to $15,000 without incurring a tax penalty. The good news? It's $15,000 per year *per* donor, so Mom and Dad could in theory gift you a total of $30,000.

Chapter 4

Tips to Help Clean Up Your Credit Score

"The best time to buy a home is always five years ago."

—Ray Brown, jazz musician

Sure, it's easy to fall in love with the idea of buying a home. You've got it all planned out: a five-bedroom home in your favorite neighborhood with a manicured lawn and—why not?—a nice pool.

But if you're going to get a mortgage (and of course, most home buyers do), you may need to improve your credit score, also called a FICO score—a simplified calculation of your history of paying back debts and making regular payments on loans. If you're borrowing money to buy a home, lenders want to know you'll pay *them* back in a timely manner, and a credit score is an easy estimate of those odds.

Here's your crash course on this all-important little number, and how to whip it into the best home-buying shape possible.

Pull your credit report

There are three major U.S. credit bureaus (Experian, Equifax, and TransUnion), and each releases its own credit scores and reports (a more detailed history that's used to determine your score). Their scores should be roughly equivalent, although they do pull from different sources. For example, Experian considers on-time rent payments, while TransUnion has detailed information about previous employers.

To get a free copy of your credit score, go to CreditKarma.com. For a free copy of your full credit report, you can get that once a year at AnnualCreditReport.com. Or check with your credit card company; some offer free access to scores and reports, says Michael Chadwick, owner of Chadwick Financial Advisors in Unionville, CT.

Once you've got your report, thoroughly review it, page by page, particularly the "adverse accounts" section, which details late payments and other slip-ups.

Assess where you stand

It's simple: The better your credit history, the higher your score—and the better your opportunities for a home loan. Major lenders often require a minimum credit score of at least 620, if not more.

So what can you do if your credit report is in less than shipshape? Don't panic, there are ways to clean it up.

How to improve your credit score with error disputes

A Federal Trade Commission (FTC) study found that 5% of credit reports contain errors that can ding your score. So if you spot any, start by sending a letter to the bureau disputing its account, providing as much documentation as possible, per FTC guidelines. You'll also need to contact the organization that provided the bad intel, such as a bank or medical provider, and ask it to update the info with the bureau. This may take a while, and you may need documentation to make your case. But once the bad info is removed, you should see your score go up.

Erase one-time mistakes

So you've made a late payment or two—who hasn't? Call the company that registered the late payment and ask that it be removed from your record.

"If you had an oopsy and missed just a payment or two, most companies will indeed tell their reporting division to remove this from your credit report," says financial planner Bob Forrest of Mutual of Omaha. Granted, this won't work if you have a history of late payments, but for accidents and small errors, it's an easy way to improve your credit score.

You can't buy a house if you have bad credit

If you're looking to get a conventional loan, having bad credit might present challenges. But FHA loans require only a 3.5% down payment, and borrowers with low credit scores—even under 600—can qualify.

Increase your limits

One no-brainer way to increase your credit score is to simply pay off your debt. Not an option right now? Here's a cool loophole: Ask your credit card companies to increase your credit limit instead. This improves your debt-to-credit ratio, which compares how much you owe to how much you can borrow.

"Having $1,000 of credit card debt is bad if you have a limit of $1,500. It isn't nearly as bad if your limit is $5,000," Forrest says. The simple math: Although you owe the same amount, you're using a much smaller percentage of your available credit, which reflects well on your borrowing practices.

Pay on time

If you're often late with payments, now's the time to change. You have the power to improve your credit score yourself. Commit to always paying your bills on time; consider signing up for automatic payments so it's guaranteed to get done.

Give yourself time

Unfortunately, negative items (such as those habitually late or nonexistent payments) can stay on your report for up to seven years. The good news? Changing your habits makes a big difference in the "payment history" segment of your report, which accounts for a large portion of your score. That's why it's essential to start early, so that you're sitting pretty once you're shopping for homes and find one that makes you swoon.

Chapter 5

How Much Home Can You Afford?

"Seven hundred and fifty grand, huh? It's not a song—it's an opera."

—Dorian Harewood, *Pacific Heights*

Knowing you want to buy a home is one thing; knowing what you can *pay for* is quite another. Too often, dreams and reality collide: You're yearning for a four-bedroom Colonial, but your wallet can handle only a two-bedroom bungalow.

So how do you find that happy medium: a home you love that's within financial reach? Not surprisingly, this hinges on how much money you're pulling in.

"The general rule of thumb is that you can purchase a home that costs two or three times your annual salary," says Harrine Freeman, a financial expert and the owner of H.E. Freeman Enterprises.

So if you're making $80,000 per year (and you have a reasonable amount of job security), that means you can afford a house up to three times that, or $240,000. That said, "This is only an estimate and does not account for your monthly bills," says Freeman. So let's dive into the specifics.

What kind of income do you need to buy a home?

According to NAR, first-time home buyers pull in a median household income of $75,000 per year. The median household income for all home buyers (first or repeat) is $91,600.

Follow the 28/36 rule

If you're overwhelmed by numbers, budgets, and big-ticket decisions, follow the 28/36 rule, a simple but effective guide for affordability. The "28" refers to your monthly housing payments—including your mortgage, insurance, and taxes—which shouldn't be more than 28% of your gross monthly income (ideally, it should be *less*). This is easy to calculate, because all you need to do is multiply. For example, if your gross monthly income (meaning before taxes are taken out) is $6,000, multiply that by 28% (or 0.28), and that means you shouldn't pay more than $1,680 a month for your home.

The "36" refers to your debt-to-income ratio, which compares how much money you owe (on credit cards, colleges, car loans, and—hopefully soon—a home loan) to your income. This ratio should be "no more than 36%," says Freeman; ideally, it should be much less.

Think about it in terms of your monthly expenses: If you make $6,000 per month but spend $500 paying off debts, you divide $500 by $6,000, to get a debt-to-income ratio of 8.3%. This is great, but adding $1,680 per month in mortgage payments would push up your monthly debt load to $2,180, and your debt-to-income ratio to 36%. This is exactly the maximum experts say you can afford. Going past this threshold is a risky move.

Once you know both these numbers, as well as how much of a down payment you plan to contribute, you can easily work out the maximum monthly mortgage payment you can afford—and by extension, the priciest house you should buy.

According to realtor.com's home affordability calculator, if you make $6,000 a month, pay $500 in debts (pre-house), and can make a down payment of $40,000, if you get a 30-year fixed mortgage at 4% interest, you can afford a house worth $277,800. Plug in your own numbers and see what happens!

POP QUIZ

How much does a starter home cost?

According to NAR, first-time home buyers spend about $203,700 for their first digs. The median home price overall (including for repeat buyers) is $250,000.

Apply for mortgage pre-approval

Another easy way to get a sense of how much home you can afford is to approach a lender and apply for mortgage pre-approval. That's where they'll take a look at your financial past and present circumstances to determine how much money they're willing to lend you to buy a home.

Just keep in mind that pre-approval is different from pre-qualification. Mortgage pre-qualification entails a basic overview of a borrower's ability to get a loan. You provide a mortgage lender with information—about your income, assets, debts, and credit—but you don't need to produce any paperwork to back it up. As such, pre-qualification is relatively easy and can be a fast way to get a ballpark figure of what you can afford. But it's by no means a guarantee that you'll actually get approved for the loan when you go to buy a home.

Getting pre-approved, in contrast, is a more in-depth process that involves a lender running a credit check and verifying your income and assets. Then an underwriter does a preliminary review of your financial portfolio and, if all goes well, issues a written commitment for financing up to a certain loan amount; this commitment is good for up to 90 or 120 days.

Moreover, getting pre-approved is typically free. Expect it to take, on average, one to three days for your application to be processed. Added bonus: Mortgage pre-approval makes you a more attractive home buyer to sellers, since they know you've got financing to back up your offer.

Factor in closing costs

Closing costs are the fees paid to third parties that help facilitate the sale of a home, and they vary widely by location. But as a rule, you can estimate that they typically total 2% to 7% of the home's purchase price. So on a $250,000 home, your closing costs would amount to anywhere from $5,000 to $17,500. Yep, that's one heck of a wide range!

Both buyers and sellers typically pitch in on closing costs, but buyers shoulder the lion's share of the load (3% to 4% of the home's price) compared with sellers (1% to 3%). Home buyers pay the majority of closing costs, since many of these fees are associated with the mortgage.

The only upfront cost is a down payment

That would be nice, but no dice. Home buyers are also responsible for closing costs, and those costs can change drastically depending on your state. And don't forget the slew of fees, taxes, and other costs for inspections, credit reports, and insurance, among other things.

Here are some of the fees home buyers should brace themselves to pay:

- A loan origination fee, which lenders charge for processing the paperwork for your loan.

- A fee for running your credit report.

- A fee for the underwriter, who assesses your creditworthiness.

- A fee for the appraisal of the home, to make sure its value matches the size of the loan you want.

- A fee for the home inspection, which checks the home for potential problems, from cracks in the foundation to a leaky roof.

- A fee for a title search to unearth any liens on the property that could interfere with your ownership of it.

- A survey fee, if it's a single-family home or townhome (but not condos).

- Taxes, also called stamp taxes, on the money you've borrowed for your home loan.

To estimate your closing costs, plug your numbers into an online closing costs calculator, or ask your real estate agent, lender, or mortgage broker for a more accurate estimate.

Consider your dreams *and* the alternatives

Once you've determined how much you can spend, you can start weighing what you absolutely *must have* in your home—and what you're willing to sacrifice if necessary. Use the "Pick 2" rule: price, quality, location. Typically, you can prioritize two of those categories, but not all three. Your best bet is to stick to an amazing neighborhood for an amazing low price, and know that your home might not have that pool, wine cellar, or other amenities you'd hoped for.

These trade-offs are just the reality of house hunting, so don't be disheartened. Consider widening your search to different neighborhoods or knocking a few items off your must-have list until you find the location and amenities that best fit your budget. Weigh what really matters for your dream home, then start performing preliminary searches online using sites such as realtor.com. And try to stay optimistic—with enough searching and some luck, you might be able to find it all.

Once you've determined what kind of house you're looking for, it's time to put your feet to the pavement and start checking out the market in person. To do that, you'll need a real estate agent.

Chapter 6

Do You Have the Right Real Estate Agent?

> "A [real estate agent] is not a salesperson. They're a matchmaker. They introduce people to homes until they fall in love with one. Then they are a wedding planner!"
>
> —Unknown

Purchasing a new home can be overwhelming, and that's why you need a comrade in arms: a close ally to steer you toward homes you'll love more than life itself, find the best possible mortgage, and help you through this emotionally and financially taxing process. That's where a good real estate agent can make a world of difference.

Not sure you want or need a real estate agent? Granted, it's true—you *can* do it on your own. But you really, really shouldn't. This is likely to be the biggest financial decision of your entire life, and you need a real estate agent if you want to do it right. Here's why.

Real estate agents have tons of experience

Want to check the MLS for a 4B/2B with an EIK and a W/D? Real estate has its own language, full of acronyms and semi-arcane jargon, and your real estate agent is trained to speak that language fluently.

Plus, buying or selling a home usually requires dozens of forms, reports, disclosures, and other technical documents. Real estate agents have the expertise to help you prepare a killer deal—while avoiding delays or costly mistakes that can seriously mess you up.

POP QUIZ

How many buyers use real estate agents, anyway?

A whole lot, since 87% of buyers purchase their home through a real estate agent or broker; 90% of buyers would use their agent again or recommend their agent to others.

They have turbocharged searching power

The internet is awesome. You can find almost anything—*anything!* And with online real estate listing sites, you can find up-to-date home listings on your own, any time you want. But guess what? Real estate agents have access to *even more* listings. Sometimes properties are available but not actively advertised. A real estate agent can help you find those hidden gems.

Plus, a good local real estate agent is going to know the search area way better than you ever could. Have your eye on a particular neighborhood, but it's just out of your price range? Your real estate agent is equipped to know the ins and outs of *every* neighborhood, so she can direct you toward a home in your price range that you may have overlooked.

They have great negotiating chops

Any time you buy or sell a home, you're going to encounter negotiations—and as today's housing market heats up, those negotiations are more likely than ever to get a little heated.

You can expect lots of competition, cutthroat tactics, all-cash offers, and bidding wars. Don't you want a savvy and professional negotiator on your side to seal the best deal for you?

And it's not just about how much money you end up spending or netting. A real estate agent will help draw up a purchase agreement that allows enough time for inspections, contingencies, and anything else that's crucial to your particular needs.

They're connected to *everyone*

Real estate agents might not know everything, but they make it their mission to know just about everyone who can possibly help in the process of buying or selling a home. Mortgage brokers, real estate attorneys, home inspectors, home stagers, interior designers, the list goes on—and they're all in your real estate agent's network. Use them.

They're your data analyst/advocate/therapist—all rolled into one

The thing about real estate agents is: They wear a lot of different hats. Sure, they're salespeople, but they actually do a whole heck of a lot to earn their commission. They're constantly driving around, checking out listings for you. They spend their own money on marketing your home (if you're selling). They're researching comps to make sure you're getting the best deal.

And, of course, they're working for you at nearly all hours of the day and night—whether you need more info on a home or just someone to talk to in order to feel at ease with the offer you've just put in. This is the most critical financial (and possibly emotional) decision of your life, and guiding you through it isn't a responsibility real estate agents take lightly.

Convinced a real estate agent can help on your home-buying journey? Here's how to find one who's got your back. And your front. Every side, actually.

Agent, broker, Realtor: What's the difference?

The first thing you might notice while trying to find home-buying help is all the different titles: agent, broker, Realtor. Are they all the same thing? Not exactly.

A real estate agent is anyone who's earned a license to sell property, which typically entails taking required course work and then passing a state exam. Brokers have continued their studies and can hire agents to work under them.

A Realtor is either an agent or broker who is a member of the National Association of Realtors. Realtors subscribe to a detailed code of ethics to treat their clients honestly and fairly. Consider it added insurance that they're committed to your cause.

Just keep in mind that these terms may vary by area. For instance, in New York state, there's no such thing as a licensed "agent" or "Realtor." Only a real estate salesperson, associate broker, or broker is licensed to sell property in New York.

Conduct a preliminary search online

We shop online for everything these days, and finding a real estate agent is no different. To locate ones in your area, use online tools such as realtor.com's Find a Realtor search, which will give you useful info, such as the agents' number of years of experience in the profession, number of homes sold, and the price of homes they typically deal with. Take note of a real estate agent's track record, because this can tip you off to superstar agents nearby and whether they're a fit for your needs.

Don't settle for good enough

According to NAR, the majority of first-time buyers found their real estate agent through a friend—and two-thirds contacted only one agent before moving forward. That's kind of like having your friends set you up on a blind date, then marrying that person by Date #2. (Hello, ugly future divorce!) After all, how can you be sure you have made the right choice without looking around? Simple: You can't.

POP QUIZ

How do buyers find their real estate agent?

It turns out 41% of buyers used an agent who was referred by a friend, neighbor or relative.

"One of the things I always tell my prospects is, 'I'm flattered if I'm the only real estate agent you are speaking to, but I think it's best if you speak with two or more so you can draw comparisons and make a powerful decision,'" says Brett West, an agent with McEnearney Associates in Washington, DC. Trust us, there can be a huge difference between an agent who's "good enough" and one who's stellar—the difference between finding your dream home or not, and saving or wasting tens of thousands of dollars.

So the extra legwork you do now could really pay off in the (not so) long term. Be sure to explore at least a few options and grill them thoroughly before settling down with one (more on that next).

Questions to ask a real estate agent

Ask *all* of these questions. This is no time for being shy! Here are some to hit:

- **How long have you been in real estate?** You're looking for a seasoned agent—and while he or she doesn't need decades of experience under her belt, less than a year or two of experience can be concerning.

- **How long have you lived in this area?** One noteworthy exception to the previous question is if the agent has lived in the area for a long time. "A newly licensed agent shouldn't be automatically removed from consideration," says Mindy Jensen, a real estate agent with Equity Colorado Real Estate. "If they've lived in the area their entire life, they likely know more about it than an agent who has been in the business for years but only recently moved to the region." Weigh overall experience against local experience when making your decision.

- **Do you have a team, or do you work alone?** Many standalone agents are excellent—but don't ignore the value of a team. "Working with a team is important," says Angelo Puma, a real estate agent in Keller, TX. "It increases response time and availability. Often, solo-run agents are double-booked when you need their attention, and you may lose that perfect property."

- **What is your schedule?** If they're not a full-time agent, you need to know when they'll be available. "If the only time you can see houses is in direct conflict with times they have to be working their other jobs, you could miss out on a lot of properties," says Jensen.

- **Do you have any vacations planned?** If they're heading out of the city anytime soon, make sure they have a backup in case you find the perfect home while they're out of the country. "Murphy's Law *rules* real estate agent vacations," says Jensen.

How are real estate agents paid?

Most real estate agent jobs are commission-only—meaning agents don't get paid a base salary by their brokerage. As a result, the amount that agents make all depends on how successful they are, which is tied to their commission.

Typically, a real estate commission is based on a percentage of a home's final sales price.

As a home buyer, you're in luck: Usually, the seller pays the real estate commission. Here's how it usually works: Commission payments go to the broker, who manages the real estate brokerage where the agent works. The commission is then split between the broker and the agent according to their agreement. The commission split varies from one agent to another, with new agents sometimes earning a smaller percentage of the commission than experienced agents or successful ones who sell more homes or more expensive properties.

The commission is split at the settlement table between the listing agent's brokerage and the buyer's agent's brokerage; then the agents themselves are paid by their brokers. So, let's say you're a home seller, and your agent charges you a 6% commission to sell your $200,000 home. The agent then has to split that 6% ($12,000) with the buyer's agent, which leaves your agent with 3% ($6,000).

But, what happens if an agent represents the buyer and the seller? In that case the agent becomes a "dual agent" and gets paid both commissions. (Talk about a big payday!) However, because it puts them in a sticky position of having to work for both the seller and buyer, many agents don't practice dual agency—and some states don't even allow it.

All of the details about a real estate agent's fee should be in the agreement you sign when you hire an agent—don't be afraid to ask questions if there's anything you don't understand.

Chapter 7

Tips for Picking the Right House

"They should put the two sections together, real estate and obituaries—Mr. Klein died today leaving a wife, two children, and a spacious three-bedroom apartment with a wood-burning fireplace."

—Billy Crystal, *When Harry Met Sally*

You've done your research, saved up for a down payment, and found a real estate agent you adore. Now comes the next step: Find your dream house already!

This is the really fun part, although it does come with its own unique challenges. Even if you love the entire process of house hunting, the options can be overwhelming. Ranch or Colonial? Suburb or city? Small apartment or palatial townhouse? Built-in 40-foot waterslide or stand-alone 40-foot waterslide? It's hard not to feel that you're drowning in the possibilities.

To help winnow the myriad options to find the perfect place for *you*, heed these tips—and happy searching!

Get pre-approved for a mortgage

Reminder: Do not even look at online listings until you have your mortgage pre-approval lined up with a lender.

"Not only will a pre-approval make it easier to eventually make an offer as a serious buyer, but it will also help you narrow down your property search criteria so you can focus better," notes Jackie Hinton, a real estate broker for Center Coast Realty in Chicago.

That's because the pre-approval letter will detail the maximum mortgage loan you're approved for, or your instant housing budget.

Have a long chat with your agent

Here's the simple truth: Only you will ultimately know which home is just right for you; however, a good agent will have a better handle on the *market*. Not only is your real estate agent keeping a constant eye out for newly listed homes you might love, but can also quickly go through your wish list and help you understand what is (and what isn't) realistic.

So be sure to tell your agent not only what you're looking for, but *why* you're moving, too.

"Are [you] downsizing? Moving closer to work? Accommodating a growing family?" asks Nathan Dart, a real estate agent in Rockville, MD. A savvy agent will point out things you might not have considered—such as the importance of a one-story home if you're near retirement and planning to stick around for the long haul.

Where do home buyers start their house hunt?

According to NAR, 44% of recent buyers start their house hunt online looking at listings on sites like realtor.com, and 17% begin by contacting a real estate agent.

Make a must-have list and stick to it

This is not as easy as it sounds, says Hinton. "Before you start looking, write down the non-negotiable features your new home needs. Then if a place doesn't have everything on the list, don't go see it, no matter how curious you are," she advises.

And the more specific the criteria, the better, contends Kate Herzig, an agent with Golston Real Estate in Arlington, VA. "For example, where I live, garages are really hard to come by, so if a garage is an absolute must-have, that is an easy way to narrow down your list of potential homes," she says.

Focusing your list has another benefit: It can help prevent "list creep," which typically occurs when you see shiny objects in each new house. If you're not careful, all of a sudden you might find your "must-have" list has grown from "3BR/2BA and a decent commute" to include a chef's kitchen—when you barely cook.

Home in on the neighborhood

Find an area that meets your criteria for amenities, commute, school district, etc., and then spend a weekend exploring before you commit, suggests Hinton.

"You might find that you don't like an area as much as you thought you would because it's impossible to find parking," she says. Or, you might discover another hidden pocket that you love and didn't realize was nearby.

Once you've taken a test drive and selected a neighborhood that you know is The One, home in on real estate listings in that specific ZIP code. This allows you to shut out a lot of the noise that can make you crazy with options.

Document your visits

Whether you're hitting open houses or scheduling showings, it's inevitable that by the fourth or fifth property, everything is going to start to blur together. Brian Wasson, an agent in Chicago, advocates keeping your smartphone handy and snapping photos from the minute you roll up to the driveway.

"Taking a picture of the 'For Sale' sign or front of the property first makes it easy to later distinguish between sets of photos," notes Wasson.

Then, as you walk through the home, capture photos of everything you like, such as a killer view or to-die-for chef's kitchen, as well as anything that feels awkward or out of place, from scary shag carpet to a funky layout. Take notes on the listing sheet so you can easily remember which features you were trying to capture in the photos, and you'll have a great play-by-play of the house to relive later.

Lessons from listings

While certain neighborhood features can boost a property's value, other features can drag down a home's price. Wondering what's the worst of the bunch? We sifted through realtor.com listings data to pinpoint neighborhood features linked to lower comparable home prices. While the list itself may not surprise you, the numbers might. Who would have thought that it's a worse investment to buy in a bad school district than near a strip club or a homeless shelter? Keep an eye out for the red flags below.

Things That Drag Down the Value of Your Home

The "drag" is calculated by comparing home prices near each facility (in the same ZIP code) with all homes in the same county.

Hospital	Shooting range	Power plant	Funeral home	Cemetery
3.2%	3.7%	5.3%	6.5%	12.3%

Homeless shelter	High renter concentration	Strip club	Bad school
12.7%	13.8%	14.7%	22.2%

realtor.com graphic

Where are Americans buying homes?

According to NAR, about 48% of Americans buy in the suburbs, followed by 20% who prefer small towns and another 20% who choose more expensive urban areas. An additional 11% settle in rural areas, while just 1% buy in resort and recreation areas.

Remember only the top three contenders

"I tell my buyers that a home is either a contender or not," says Brian Adams, real estate agent with StarPointe Realty in Killeen, TX. In other words, either it's one of your current top three properties or you should forget about it. This simple trick means you have to keep only three homes in mind at a time.

Don't worry about timing

Patience is difficult. You want your new home *right away*. Waiting for something to fall into place can feel like endless purgatory. But that doesn't mean you should rush the hunt.

"I've had clients who spend years in house-hunting mode," says Gretchen Koitz, a real estate agent with the Koitz Group in Bethesda, MD. Not that this is a good thing either, but our point is this: Don't rush it if you don't have to.

How long will the house hunt take?

According to NAR, buyers typically search for homes for about 10 weeks and visit 10 homes before they make an offer.

See beyond the decor

Many people are flat-out terrible decorators, and you're allowed to initially be turned off by an ugly home. But you shouldn't let stylistic choices affect your judgment of what a home *could* be. As Koitz puts it, "'I hate the red paint in the dining room' is not a valid concern." Look beyond those garish drapes to the bones beneath. Is the picture window hidden behind them stunning? Is the hardwood floor good quality, despite the stained rugs layered on top? Think of the long term. Remember, the current owners' raggedy stuff will leave with them.

Tune in to how you feel

Not to get too woo-woo spiritual about it, but house hunting isn't just about what you see. It's also about how you *feel*.

"A big part of home buying is pure emotion," says Koitz. And this swirl of feelings may surprise you, drawing you toward homes you never thought you'd love and away from ones that hit every box on your checklist.

"Agents have a secret saying, which is that 'Buyers are liars,'" says Koitz. "We don't mean that buyers really mean to lie, but that what they think they want in a home often goes out the window when emotion kicks in."

Don't forget your must-have list, but don't feel bad about skipping something you *thought* you wanted. A wonderful house without a his-and-her bathroom is still a wonderful house—you just might have to shuffle your expectations.

"It's important for buyers to keep in mind that there is no such thing as the perfect house," Dart says. "At the end of the day, you'll find some place that hits the high notes and that includes the things that were most important to you."

Schools don't matter if you don't have kids

The neighborhood you choose matters—both now and later, when you might consider selling. Even if you don't have children, good schools are a sign of a good neighborhood. Also, check out the area's walkability, your commute to work, and any other features that would make the 'hood a good fit for your lifestyle—now and a decade from now.

Lessons from listings

Curious which amenities are highly valued in a home today? Here are a few desirable features based on realtor.com listings data, and how quickly homes with them get snapped up:

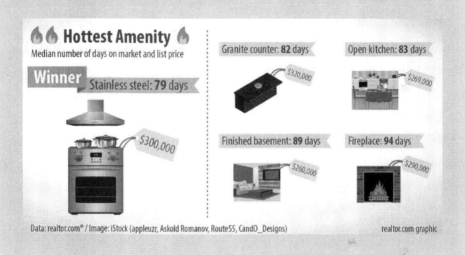

🔥🔥 **Hottest Amenity** 🔥
Median number of days on market and list price

Winner Stainless steel: **79** days
$300,000

Granite counter: **82** days
$320,000

Open kitchen: **83** days
$269,000

Finished basement: **89** days
$260,000

Fireplace: **94** days
$290,000

Data: realtor.com® / Image: iStock (appleuzr, Askold Romanov, Route55, CandO_Designs)   realtor.com graphic

What kinds of houses are out there, anyway?

Now that you have a sense of what you should be searching for, let's dive into the fun part: A guide to all the types of homes you'll see! Here's a guide to the most popular architecture styles to help you identify what you want in your house hunt.

Cape Cod

OK, it's no spoiler that these homes are named after the quintessential New England vacation destination—Cape Cod in Massachusetts—where they first became prevalent. Much like the Puritans of old, Cape Cod homes are modest and economical. This makes sense, since Colonial settlers in the Northeast modeled their homes after British cottages. These homes have steep roofs that reach the first floor (to quickly shed rain and snow) and second-story dormers (a window

that projects vertically from a sloping roof). Fun fact: Original Capes used unfinished cedar shingles, which are ideal to weather the stormy and unforgiving East Coast winters.

Colonial

A Colonial is symmetrical and features an entry door in the middle of the front of the home with two windows on either side; there are five windows on the second floor, with one directly above the entry door. They're usually built of wood or brick, which are perfectly suited to the

simple, clean, and boxy style. Colonials originally rose in popularity in the 1700s, and are still common around the United States. In fact, they're considered one of America's most "traditional" styles.

Victorian

Did you spend hours with your dollhouse as a kid? Then the detail-packed Victorian style will probably look familiar. Key features include a complicated, asymmetrical shape with wings and bays in various directions; elaborate trim; shingles or patterned masonry; steep rooflines; and a large, wraparound porch. They are often painted in

bright, complementary colors to highlight the painstaking details. Some people are put off by their aggressive whimsy, but plenty consider them perfect houses to grow old in and sip lemonade on the porch.

Tudor

Tudors are built of brick or stone on the first level and complementary stucco and timbering on the second—all of which is inspired by the architecture of Tudor England in the early 16th century. These babies

are made to withstand the elements, with deeply pitched roofs and detailed, covered entryways, which is why you'll see more of them in the chilly Northeast.

Ranch

Blame (or credit, depending on how you feel about this style) the rise of the automobile, not cowboys, for ranch houses. Cars made it possible for families to buy large lots of land outside traditional metropolitan centers—aka "the suburbs"—so people built spread-out ranch houses to take advantage of these new spaces. These homes are one story and

often have an L- or U-shaped floor plan surrounding a patio, sliding glass doors, and a carport or garage. Quite possibly the best-known symbol of American housing—no doubt you'll see lots of them.

Bungalow

These adorable one-story homes are characterized by their low, pitched roofs and large front porches. Also called Craftsmans, they rose in popularity in the early 1900s during the Arts and Crafts period and were revered for their—you guessed it—handcrafted details: hand-cut

wood, iron and copper work, and masonry. Bungalows hit their peak during this period and became so popular in the early part of the past century that you could order a complete kit from Sears.

Spanish

You find a lot of these homes in the South or Southwest (Hollywood is full of them). One reason for their popularity: They're built from the ground up to take the heat. Clay tile roofs keep the home cool

during the hot summer months and extend beyond the walls to provide extra shade, while extensive outdoor living areas, columns, and arched windows and openings take advantage of the breeze.

Midcentury modern

Full of sharp angles and void of ornamentation, these contemporary homes offer flat or shallow-pitched roofs and loads of glass. They often incorporate the surrounding outdoor space via decks and balconies.

While they started sprouting on the landscape in the 1950s, their timeless aesthetic has turned these sleek, stripped-down houses into classics.

French Country

The French Country/Provincial style was inspired by the rustic manors that dotted the fields of northern and southern France during the reign of Louis XIV in the 17th century. The Revival style popped up in the 1920s and 1960s. The homes often have a square shape with windows

(often double windows and/or balconies) balanced on either side of the entrance and a steep, hipped roof. They are most often made of stone, stucco, and brick.

Condos, townhouses, and duplexes

While the vast majority of home buyers (82%) purchase a detached, single-family house, that's not your only option. Eight percent purchase a townhouse or row house, which are homes that share at least one wall with other dwellings. Four percent buy condos (private residences within larger buildings) or duplexes (two residences in one building). Townhouses, row houses, condos and duplexes are often found in more densely populated urban areas where space is at a premium. If you enjoy being in the thick of things, and don't mind having neighbors right on top (or to the side) of you, then these more densely built dwellings may be just right for you.

Lessons from listings

Wondering which architectural styles are most popular today? Based on our analysis of realtor.com listings data, here's how long certain home styles sit on the market before buyers bite.

🔥🔥 **Hottest Style** 🔥
Median number of days on market and list price

Winner Spanish: **47** days

$550,000

Traditional: **84** days
$233,000

Ranch: **95** days
$179,000

Craftsman: **103** days
$350,000

Victorian: **122** days
$259,000

Data: realtor.com® / Image: Pop Chart Lab   realtor.com graphic

Plus: The 6 *worst* homes for first-time buyers

While only you will know the right house for you, take it from us—some homes just aren't right for the average first-time buyer. So make sure to keep these clunkers on your radar before you make a purchase you might regret.

The home that's a little too cozy

You may not have children when you buy your first house. You may not even be planning on having children. But those plans could change in the next five to 10 years, and that tiny two-bedroom historic bungalow you've been eyeing may go from just right to clown-car small.

"If you are recently married and plan to start a family, do *not* buy a two-bedroom home. Unless you bunk the kids together, you will be moving once the second child comes along," says Seth Lejeune, a real estate agent with Berkshire Hathaway HomeServices in Collegeville, PA. "Three-bedroom is generally a good thing to start with if a family is in the cards."

The bloater

On the flip side, you shouldn't just get the biggest house you can qualify for, either. Five bedrooms might make sense for you in the future, but if it's just you and your partner now, you probably won't need those other four bedrooms for *years*. In the meantime, you'll be carrying a much larger mortgage than you need—or possibly can handle.

"There's almost nothing worse than buying more house than you need and having a reminder come in the mail every month as you scrounge to make payments," Lejeune says.

The money pit

You might be tempted to buy an older fixer-upper—after all, you've watched so much HGTV you could give Chip Gaines a run for his (considerable) money—but be careful how much rehab you take on.

If the home needs one or two biggish projects and a handful of small weekend jobs to get into perfect condition, you might come out ahead. But if you can spot a dozen problem areas now, you may end up going broke trying to repair that place.

Instead, opt for a fixer-upper with an end in sight.

"I generally advise people to keep it simple—like kitchens and bath upgrades," Lejeune says.

The weekend stealer

Is the front lawn a tropical garden? Does the house have a swimming pool out back? Is there a huge vegetable garden that needs tending? Those features might look great now, but do you really want to spend every weekend maintaining your home?

"Pools, hot tubs, elaborate landscaping, etc. are great in theory, but all require maintenance," Lejeune says.

If you're not up for the challenge, move right along. Nothing to see here, folks.

The dream crusher

In an ideal world, you'll live in your first home for a while, maybe make a few improvements, and sell it for a profit later so you can upgrade to an even more awesome pad.

But that doesn't mean you should look at every home solely for its investment potential.

Sometimes your tireless home improvements won't mean much to the next buyer. And sometimes that home simply isn't going to go up in price, no matter how many improvements you make.

If your only reason for making an offer is what you might get out of it after you sell it, consider the market very, *very* carefully before you make the plunge.

The doorbuster

If you've found a really good deal on a home, go ahead and pat yourself on the back for being a regular real estate pro. But then stop and ask yourself why the deal's so great. Is the location a bit gritty? You might save big bucks in the beginning, but there also might be big problems if and when you try to sell the home later on.

"I would advise that you pick [a location] with a strong school district and a fiscally sound municipality," Lejeune says.

Even if you don't plan on having children, or you don't care if a neighborhood is a little rough around the edges, future buyers might—and that means you may be forced to offer the same discount you got when you bought the house. And nobody wants their decisions as a first-time buyer to come back and haunt them as a first-time seller.

Chapter 8

How to Make an Offer on a House

"Home is the nicest word there is."

—Laura Ingalls Wilder

We'll get right down to it: Shopping for a home is fun. But once you find "The One," things start to get real—*real* fast. Think of making an offer on a home as setting the roller coaster in motion: You might have sharp drops in emotion and slow, trudging climbs to success, but the ride won't end until the car slows down and the safety bar is lifted. (OK, this metaphor is now officially over.)

You need to learn how to make the right offer, the one that will end with your receiving the keys to your new house. So check out some of these agent-approved negotiation tactics to make the process a whole lot less bumpy.

Pick the right price

Just because the home is listed at $300,000 doesn't mean it's actually worth that much. It all depends on the market. If you're buying somewhere hot—especially in places with low inventory—offering substantially below asking price is "probably wasting your time," says Mindy Jensen, a real estate agent with Equity Colorado. But if the place has been sitting unsold for a few months, even the sellers probably don't expect full price. Your best reality gauge is to check out comparables, or "comps." This is what nearby homes of similar size have sold for recently.

REAL ESTATE MYTH

A home's list price is set in stone

Much like buying a car, the offer you make on a house does not need to be the asking price. If you have stellar credit, pre-approval, and a down payment ready to go, sellers might be more willing to negotiate than to wait for another, possibly less awesome, buyer to come around.

Work with your real estate agent to determine a fair asking price; he or she will have the best read on pricing and marketplace dynamics, and can walk through the comps with you. Your agent can help you determine what a fair discount would be without offending the seller. While specific numbers will depend on your market, experts estimate that it's unrealistic to go below 5% of the list price unless it's been sitting on the market for months. Which leads us to...

Lowball with care

Sometimes a home is priced just too high—no ifs, ands, or buts. Or maybe it's been sitting unsold for half a year. In those situations, an offer well under asking price might be the right strategy to get the home you love at a bargain price. However, this is a tool to be deployed rarely and with great care, especially if the current owners have lived there for many years.

"Longtime owners usually have tons of pride in their home, and want the new owners to love it like they do," says Jodie Burns, a real estate agent with McEnearney Associates. "Buyers who lowball run a risk of angering the seller and losing the house. Ideally, you're looking for a closing where both sides feel like they got a fair deal."

So don't lowball unless both you and your real estate agent agree that it's the best strategy for the occasion. Think about the big picture: "If a couple of thousand dollars is going to keep them out of a home they love, I remind buyers how little that amount translates into a monthly payment," Burns says.

Pony up some earnest money

Also known as "good-faith money," earnest money is a sum put up by the buyer and generally held in escrow or trust to show the buyer is serious about purchasing the home. There is no defined amount, but earnest money generally runs at about 1% to 2% of the purchase price.

When the purchase is complete, that money is applied toward your down payment or closing costs. If the contract doesn't go through, there are guidelines that vary by state that determine which party will be awarded that money. One way to get back your earnest money is to add contingencies to your offer (more on that next).

Write a letter

If the market's tight and you've decided that you *must* have that stunning Colonial, you can boost your chances by writing a personal letter.

"Top dollar will typically win the bid, but the sellers get to choose which offer they like best," says Jensen. "Including a letter can sway them toward you, or at least give you the opportunity to match the highest offer."

Jensen recommends scouting the house to figure out what's important to the sellers and mentioning it in your letter. For example, a dog shed in the backyard means they're probably canine lovers—and more likely to respond to your excitement over little Humbert's potential new backyard. If they're mountain bikers, they'll love that you're excited about the nearby trails, too. And, of course, parents who raised their (now grown-up) kid-dos in this home will appreciate your intention to do the same.

Just keep in mind that some real estate professionals do not recommend writing such a letter, so make sure to discuss this with your real estate agent first.

REAL ESTATE MYTH

Cash is king

Cash offers bring one big benefit to a home seller: Since no loan is needed to finance this purchase, this greases the wheels to a smooth sale without any hiccups. But on the flip side, that myth assumes that sellers care most about a fast and certain close, and that's not always true. Often, if you make the bigger offer, or you write a killer personal letter that resonates with the seller, you stand a better chance of getting approved over an all-cash offer.

Consider contingencies

Along with the price, you'll also want to factor contingencies into your contract. Contingencies are requirements that must be met before a real estate deal can close, set and agreed upon by the buyer and seller. The sellers, for instance, might have a contingency that they must sell their home before you can move in. For a buyer, here are some of the most common contingencies you'll want to consider:

Home inspection contingency: This gives buyers the right to have the home professionally inspected. If anything falls short, you can request that it be fixed—or you can back out of the sale. It's rarely advisable to waive an inspection contingency. Although the average home inspection costs $300 to $500, it's a drop in the bucket considering the costly home issues it might uncover.

Financing contingency: This contingency gives you the right to back out of the deal if your mortgage approval falls through. You have a specified time period, as stated in the sales contract, during which you have to obtain a loan that will cover the mortgage.

Home appraisal contingency: With this contingency, a third party hired by your mortgage lender evaluates the fair market value of the home. If the appraised value is less than the sale price, the contingency enables you to back out of the deal without forfeiting your earnest money deposit.

There are more contingencies to consider, and they all serve to protect your interests, so work with your real estate agent to decide what you'll ask for off the bat. That said, since contingencies can slow down a sale, consider dropping some requests if the market is hot. As Jensen explains, "Your chances are best if you ask for the fewest things." Don't put yourself at risk to get the home you love, though. Some people might advocate dropping the inspection clause to sweeten your offer, but that can be dangerous, especially with older homes.

Keep your emotions in check

Yes, the search seems to have dragged on forever; *yes*, this home has everything you need. But keep your wits about you.

"Don't fall in love," Jensen says. "Falling in head over heels with a home can make you do ridiculous things. Like overpay."

And sometimes, even an "excellent offer may not be accepted," says Vici Boguess, a real estate agent with the Burke Boguess Zimmerman Group in Alexandria, VA. Don't assume a rejection is an insult—the sellers might just dislike some of your contingencies or be holding out for a better offer. So, don't assume it's over until it's over.

Plus: 6 things you should never say when buying a home

While you can (and should) always be upfront with your real estate agent, you might not want to be quite so candid around the sellers (or the listing agent working for them). The reason? Just like in *Law & Order*, what you say can—and will—be used against you. So before you stick your foot in your mouth, during your house hunt or your negotiations, consider these bloopers that you should never say to sellers or their agents.

"This is my dream house!"

Do you ever play poker? Well, then, you should know that if you want to maintain a strong negotiating position, never tip your hand, advises New Jersey real estate agent Ryan Gibbons. Interested parties who express their unbridled passion for a home are shooting themselves in the foot.

"These are the kind of things that can help the sellers snag more money out of the buyers, because they really know how much this house means to them," he notes. "All discussions about the house and any negotiating strategies are best left in private." Not that you shouldn't say a few nice things—just don't gush. Gushing = bad.

"That couch is hideous"

"Don't tell the sellers—or any agent present—that they have poor taste in decor or furniture," says Naveed Shah, a real estate agent in McLean, VA, with Keller Williams. "Their style might not suit yours, but that's no reason to insult them. If they hear you bad-mouthing their rug or curtains, then they might just pick another buyer."

"I can afford to spend *x*"

While it's certainly a good idea for prospective buyers to find out just how much they can afford, they should keep that intel strictly between them and their real estate agent.

"A prospective home buyer should *never* address with a seller or seller's agent anything concerning their financing or ability to pay a full-price offer," says Maryjo Shockley, a real estate agent with Keller Williams in Wellington, FL. "This hampers the ability to negotiate the fairest price for the property." If asked, just say, "Finding a fairly priced home is what matters to us more than the amount we can afford." It works!

"I can't wait to get rid of that"

Even if you're thinking, "This place will be perfect once I get my hands on it," don't let on, notes Betsy Bingle, an associate broker with Linton Bingle Associate Brokers in Jackson, WY.

"If the new buyers are going to renovate a home in which someone raised a family and has truckloads of memories, a buyer should never say 'I can't wait to rip that swing set out' or 'That wall color is horrible—can't wait to repaint this place,'" she says.

"The seller can easily reject their offer or come back asking for more money, upon hearing that someone wants to totally remake the place where they made lifelong memories," she adds.

"Why are you selling?"

Yes, you may very well be curious to find out why sellers have put their home on the market. Keep it to yourself! It's considered poor taste to ask, and it may open a can of worms.

"Never ask the sellers why they are selling," explains real estate agent Klara Madlin of Klara Madlin Real Estate in New York. "There may be personal reasons like divorce or a job relocation or something worse—none of it your business." Opening up a possibly uncomfortable situation will not help you down the road should a bidding war emerge.

"You'll never get that price!"

Although you might be thinking "I wouldn't give them x amount for that house," as a buyer, it's best for you to keep your thoughts and opinions to yourself, notes Cara Ameer, a real estate agent with Coldwell Banker in Ponte Vedra Beach, FL. Even if a buyer thinks a home is priced on the high side, it could very well be within the range of comparables in the neighborhood.

Bottom line? It's never wise to insult the person whose home you're trying to buy.

Chapter 9

How to Land a Great Home Loan

"People are living longer than ever before, a phenomenon undoubtedly made necessary by the 30-year mortgage."

—Doug Larson, columnist

If you're shopping for a home, odds are you're shopping for a mortgage as well. In the entire home-buying process, it's perhaps the most intimidating step: convincing a bank to hand you hundreds of thousands of dollars. How do you pull it off? And what strings are attached?

These days, finding a home loan is by no means a one-mortgage-fits-all model. Where you live, how long you plan to stay put, and other variables can make certain home loans better suited to your circumstances, and choosing wisely could save you a bundle on your down payment, fees, and interest.

To learn about all your options, check out these common types of home loans and whom they're suited for, so you can make the right choice.

How many home buyers need a mortgage?

Since most of us aren't sitting on piles of cash, the vast majority of home buyers (88%) need a home loan to finance their purchase.

Fixed-rate loan

The most common type of loan, a fixed-rate loan prescribes a single interest rate—and monthly payment—for the life of the loan, which is typically 15 or 30 years.

Right for: homeowners who crave predictability and aren't going anywhere soon. You pay x amount for y years—and that's the end of it. The rise and fall of interest rates (like the nationwide increase that followed the Fed's action in December 2018) won't change the terms of your loan, so you'll always know what to expect. That said, fixed-rate loans are best for people who plan to stay in their home for at least a good chunk of the life of their loan; if you think you'll move fairly soon, you may want to consider the next option.

Adjustable-rate mortgage (ARM)

ARM loans offer interest rates typically lower than you'd get with a fixed-rate loan for a period of time—such as five or 10 years. But after that, your interest rates (and payments) will adjust, typically once a year, roughly corresponding to current interest rates. So if interest rates shoot up, so do your monthly payments; if they plummet, you'll pay less.

Right for: home buyers with lower credit scores. Since people with poor credit typically can't get good rates on fixed-rate loans, an ARM can nudge those interest rates down enough to put homeownership within easier reach. These loans are also great for people who plan to move and sell their home before their fixed-rate period is up and their rates start fluctuating.

Federal Housing Administration (FHA) loan

While typical loans require a down payment of 20% of the purchase price of your home, with a Federal Housing Administration loan, you can put down as little as 3.5%.

Right for: home buyers with meager savings for a down payment. These loans come with several caveats. First, most loans are limited to $417,000 and don't provide much flexibility: Rates are typically fixed, with either 15- or 30-year terms. Buyers are also required to pay mortgage insurance—either upfront or over the life of the loan—which hovers at around 1% of the cost of your loan.

U.S. Department of Agriculture (USDA) loan

USDA Rural Development loans are designed for families in rural areas. The government finances 100% of the home price—in other words, no down payment is necessary—and offers discounted interest rates to boot.

Right for: families in rural areas who are struggling financially. These loans are designed to put homeownership within their grasp. The catch? Your debt load cannot exceed your income by more than 41%, and, just as for the FHA loan, you will be required to purchase mortgage insurance.

Veterans Affairs (VA) loan

If you've served in the United States military, a Veterans Affairs loan can be an excellent alternative to a traditional mortgage. If you qualify, you can score a sweet home with no money down and no mortgage insurance requirements.

Right for: veterans who've served 90 days consecutively during wartime, 180 during peacetime, or six years in the reserves. That said, the VA has strict requirements for the type of home you can purchase: It must be your primary residence, and it must meet "minimum property requirements" (that is, no fixer-uppers are allowed).

Still not sure which loan is right for you? Here are some additional questions to ask yourself—and the answers you need—to help you ace this all-important step.

Should you work with a bank or a broker?

Many home buyers get their mortgage directly from a bank—often the institution where they're stashing their primary savings. But that's hardly your only, or best, option. Shopping around with different lenders may land you a better deal (typically in the form of a lower interest rate—you can comparison shop interest rates at realtor.com/mortgage).

Or you can choose to hire a pro—a mortgage broker.

Brokers work directly with lenders to negotiate terms and determine the best loans for *you*—not the generic "you," but you *specifically*, taking into account your needs, income, savings, and any special situations that might apply. For instance, first-time buyers might have just landed a better job or gotten a raise, giving you more buying power that isn't reflected in the last two years of your tax documents. The right broker will be able to find loans that take only the past year's returns into account.

The downside? Brokers may charge a fee. While many receive this fee from the lender, they might also charge you, too. Still, if your financial situation is complex or you lack the time to do your own research, paying a broker could be money well spent.

Should you get a mortgage for 15 or 30 years?

Most mortgages offer two options: for 15 or for 30 years. A 15-year loan offers a lower interest rate but higher monthly payments, since you're paying it off in half the time. Conversely, a 30-year loan offers lower monthly payments, but you'll pay more interest over those 30 years.

So which one is right for you? That depends on what you can afford. But consider this: Over the life of the loan, a 30-year mortgage means you'll end up paying a lot more in interest than you would with a 15-year mortgage. That's because essentially, with a 30-year loan, you're borrowing the same amount of money for twice as long—at a higher interest rate.

Should you get a loan online or in person?

Online mortgage lenders such as LendingTree and Quicken Loan's Rocket Mortgage allow home buyers to complete the entire mortgage application on their laptop or phone, rather than heading to a bank to submit all that paperwork in person.

While it's hard to beat online mortgages in terms of convenience, home buyers should know that there are both advantages and disadvantages to financing a home purchase in this manner. The pros? For one, you can easily comparison shop and get a loan quickly— Quicken Loan's Rocket Mortgage, for instance, boasts that it can whiz you through the application process in a mere 8 minutes.

The cons? Because most online lenders are national entities, many of them don't employ mortgage specialists who know the ins and outs of your local market. This can be a big disadvantage if you're applying for a complicated loan, such as an FHA loan or a mortgage for a self-employed borrower. Also, online mortgage lenders aren't typically as well-versed in local home buyer's incentive programs, and such programs can help drive down your interest rate or reduce your closing fees. So if your own situation is a bit more outside-the-box, you may have more alternatives with a local lender or broker.

Should you lock in your rate now or later?

A lock allows you to fix a specific interest rate for a specified length of time before closing. This protects you if market rates go higher.

Or you can add a float-down—an extra feature that can be added to a lock. It allows you the flexibility to get an even lower rate if rates happen to retreat after a lock is set.

These features require a fee, but depending on the volatility of the market and how critical it is for you to keep down your monthly mortgage payment, that cash could be a worthwhile investment.

Can you negotiate anything?

You may not have much luck negotiating the interest rate or terms of the loan, but there are other areas where lenders might be willing to give you more wiggle room.

"Ask for an itemized list of expenses, and see what's up for debate," says Anne Postic, the editor of Mortgages.com. Pay attention to the little charges. "Do you see a courier or mail fee, but you did everything electronically?" Postic says. "Those fees may be standard for your lender, and they can be waived."

Lenders might also be willing to waive the application fee or pay some of your closing costs, decreasing your costs overall. Mortgage brokers can be helpful here, so make sure to talk to them about lowering any added expenses and fees.

Chapter 10

The Home Appraisal Process

"There have been few things in my life which have had a more genial effect on my mind than the possession of a piece of land."

—Harriet Martineau, sociologist

You've found the house you love, had your offer accepted, and even locked in a mortgage! Time to break out the Dom Pérignon White Gold? Sorry, not yet.

If you've applied for a mortgage, your home-to-be still has to undergo a home appraisal. Lenders require this to know that the money they're loaning you is heading to a sound investment. In fact, an unfavorable appraisal can kill a deal.

Yikes! It can be a nerve-wracking ordeal, but it's actually good for you. Honest. Allow us to demystify the process.

Appraisals estimate a home's value with fresh eyes

While the home appraisal process is a process that is somewhat similar to getting comps—as you did to determine a fair price—appraisers delve in, in much more detail, to determine the home's exact value.

They'll investigate the condition, the square footage, location, and any additions or renovations. Another key difference is that when you looked at the comps, you were probably hoping for a specific outcome—perhaps even some flaw that you could use as a bargaining chip to lower the price.

Appraisers, on the other hand, are trained to be unbiased, says Adam Wiener, the founder of Aladdin Appraisal in Auburndale, MA. "I don't care what anybody wants the home to be worth," he says. "I'll give you the answer. You may not like it, but it's the answer."

An appraisal is the same thing as a home inspection

Although both the appraisal and the home inspection are used as safeguards for the buyer (and the buyer's lender), don't confuse the two. Home inspectors and appraisers have completely different tasks. Sure, they both poke around a home. But the inspector's job is to uncover everything that's problematic—or could potentially become problematic—with the home, while the appraiser's job is to find the objective market value of the property.

You'll get a copy of the appraisal, too

Appraisers set out to determine if the home is actually worth what you're planning to pay. You might be surprised how little time that takes; they could be in and out of a home in 30 minutes, and that's not a reason to panic.

Appraisers aren't home inspectors, who examine every little detail. While they'll pay particular attention to problems with the foundation and roof, the home appraisal process includes noting the quality and condition of the appliances, plumbing, flooring, and electrical system. With data in hand, they make their final assessment and give their report to the lender. The mortgage company is then required by law to give a copy of the appraisal to you.

Appraisers work for your lender—not you

As the buyer, you'll be paying for the home appraisal. In most cases, the fee is wrapped into your closing costs and will set you back only $300 to $400. However, just because you pay doesn't mean you're the client.

"My client is the lender, not the buyer," Wiener says. This ensures that appraisers remain ethical—in fact, it's a crime to coerce or put any pressure on an appraiser to hit a certain value. Appraisers must remain independent. "Anything less, and public trust in the appraisal is lost," says Wiener.

They still protect buyers from a bad deal

In essence, the home appraisal process is meant to protect you (and the lender) from a bad purchase. For instance: If the appraisal comes in higher than the price you'd agreed to pay, it's generally fine. Sure, the sellers could decide they want more money and would rather put their home back on the market, but in most cases, the deal will go through as expected.

If your appraisal comes in lower than what you have offered, this is where things get tricky: Your lender won't pony up more money than the appraised price. So if you and the sellers agree on $125,000 but the appraisal comes in at $105,000, it creates a $20,000 shortfall. What's a buyer to do? Read on.

Appraisal came in low? What to do

The home-buying process is a high-stakes thrill ride full of exhilarating ups and scary downs, but unquestionably one of the most deflating moments is when the appraisal comes in significantly lower than the accepted offer. So, what do you do if this happens to you? You have four options:

1. Appeal the appraisal

Sometimes called a "rebuttal of value," the appraisal appeal takes some work. In fact, it's a total team effort.

"The homeowner, loan officer, and often the real estate agent work together to find better comparable market data to justify a higher valuation," says mortgage adviser Casey Fleming.

That means everyone puts on their best Sherlock Holmes garb and gets to work looking for anything that supports the claim for a higher valuation. Perhaps the appraiser overlooked some comps (homes similar in style, location, and square footage, sold within the past few years).

"It's not uncommon to discover, for instance, that the appraiser used a comparable sale that looks like it's in great condition, when, in fact, the home was trashed when purchased and has already been rehabilitated," Fleming says.

The loan officer writes an appeal using the new comparables and then sends it to the appraiser. There might be some negotiating back and forth until all parties agree on a compromise and a new valuation.

2. Get a second appraisal

"Most often, if the appraised value is not as high as the agreed price, the seller's agent will ask to see the comps and get a second or third appraisal," says Diane Saatchi, a senior broker with Saunders & Associates in Bridgehampton, NY.

But it will cost you—you're paying for all of those additional appraisals as well. They can range between a few hundred dollars and $1,000, depending on the area. Occasionally, real estate agents or sellers will foot the bill if they really want to keep the sale.

3. Negotiate with the seller

If you're lucky, both you and the seller will budge a little.

"You might go back to the sellers and ask them to reduce the price or split the difference," says Peter Grabel, managing director of Luxury Mortgage in Stamford, CT. "The seller is under no obligation to do so, but they may prefer to do this rather than take a chance of losing you as a buyer, and starting over again. It is likely that another buyer will have the same issue, so the sellers might be better off renegotiating with you, unless they have other offers."

Sellers might be more willing to cooperate, especially if the Federal Housing Administration is involved. Lenders often require the use of their own FHA-approved appraiser, and these appraisals are "locked in" for six months.

"The seller could be forced to take a poor appraisal or wait it out for a buyer with a different loan," explains Joshua Jarvis of Jarvis Team Real Estate in Duluth, GA.

Jeff Knox, broker and owner of Dallas-area real estate firm Knox & Associates, says this is the most common outcome in his area.

"Of all possible outcomes, this is what happens most frequently," he says. "While the seller will usually be upset about the low appraisal value, most reasonable sellers eventually come to terms with the fact that any other appraisal values by potential future buyers will most likely come in at about the same value."

4. Walk away

No one wants to let a property slip through their fingers, especially if it feels like their dream home. But beware of ignoring a low appraisal—you could end up losing thousands when you decide to sell.

If you have an appraisal contingency in your contract, you can walk away, get your deposit back, and hope for better luck the next time around.

Chapter 11

All About the Home Inspection

"Here lies Walter Fielding. He bought a house. And it killed him."

—Tom Hanks, *The Money Pit*

A home inspection can be a terrifying process to newbie buyers: What if the house you adore has major problems hiding beneath that shiny new coat of paint? If you lie awake haunted by visions of mold or foundation issues, it's time to take a deep breath. Here's everything you need to know about home inspections, and how (as scary as they might seem) they exist to protect you from a very bad deal.

Here are some insights into how to make the most of this all-important step.

What does a home inspector check out?

A whole lot! The National Association of Home Inspectors' checklist of things to vet include 1,600 different items within a home. Home inspectors use these lists while inspecting homes, and while they may vary by individual and geographic area, rest assured, this list is incredibly long—proving that a whole lot can go wrong with a home!

Here's a rundown of the main things a home inspection checklist will include:

☑ **Structural issues**: "Your home must properly support the weight of its own structure," says Jeffrey Miller, real estate agent and team lead at AE Home Group in Baltimore. "Over time, critical elements may begin to fail." A home inspector will look for a cracked foundation, sagging beams, wood rot, and uneven floors, identifying areas that may be compromised.

☑ **Roof problems**: If the roof is sloped, Miller says, an inspector will look for curling or missing shingles, worn granules, cracks in skylight sealant, loose gutters, etc. If the roof is flat, the inspector will want to check for cracks in the seams and any divots or spongy areas.

"They're looking for any signs that that roof is no longer structurally sound or may allow in water in the near future," Miller notes.

☑ **Mechanical issues**: From central air to water radiators, the heating and cooling systems in a house should be turned on by the inspector (regardless of the season) to ensure they're in proper working condition.

☑ **Plumbing concerns**: Although a home inspector can inspect only plumbing that is visually accessible, the checklist will include keeping an eye out for leaks under bathroom sinks, signs of corrosion and rusting of cast-iron drain lines, and water pressure.

☑ **Electrical troubles**: Electrical issues could spark house fires, which is why inspectors check outlets individually to ensure they're properly hooked up to power and grounded. They'll also check for code violations and gauge the age of the electrical system.

☑ **Overall condition**: Do the doors stick? Are there windows that have been painted shut? Will the oven that is being sold with the house actually turn on? A home inspector's checklist includes walking through the house and checking on these basic elements, so that issues can be rectified before you buy.

☑ **Safety**: The home inspection checklist will include items that may compromise the safety of you and your family. That list includes the following:

- Open stair risers that are too high
- Wobbly deck supports
- Loose or missing handrails
- Nonfunctional smoke and carbon monoxide detectors
- Peeling paint if the home was built before 1978
- Signs of mold
- Spongy subfloors
- Tripping hazards
- Signs that a chimney needs maintenance

How to hire a top-notch home inspector

While it may be tempting to hire any run-of-the-mill home inspector to get the job done—particularly if the price is right—the inspection is no time to cut corners. After all, buying a home is an enormous investment. "Everyone does themselves a disservice when they shop by price alone," says Alan Singer of Sterling Home Inspections in Armonk, NY. "Plenty of inspectors don't know what they're doing and set up shop because it's easy to do."

So, first, check your local requirements: Many states require an inspector to have a license or insurance, and not having either is a big, waving red flag. Even if insurance is not mandated, you're better off choosing an inspector who *is* insured, which protects both of you against errors and omissions. Membership in a professional trade organization, such as the American Society of Home Inspectors, indicates that the inspector is up to date on the latest developments in the field—another giant plus.

REAL ESTATE MYTH

Brand-new homes don't need to be inspected

Faulty construction can lead to all kinds of repair nightmares, so sparkly new houses need to be checked—maybe even more carefully than older ones. "With a house that's already been lived in, I can see whether there are signs of leakage, mold, or anything that occurs over a period of time," explains Frank Lesh, executive director of the American Society of Home Inspectors. "If it's a brand-new house, nobody has showered in that shower or used the appliances, so it absolutely should be inspected, even though it's under warranty."

Why you should attend the home inspection

Even though you will receive a written report after the home inspection, you should attend the inspection while it's being done. It provides a valuable opportunity to learn all about the inner workings of your would-be new home.

"I much prefer it when buyers are there, so we can discuss the home in person," Singer says. "It's much easier to explain the ramifications of an issue when we're standing in front of it." Plus, it sure beats deciphering a 10-page report about heating, ventilation, and air-conditioning (HVAC) or plumbing problems.

So, don't be afraid to ask questions. Really stick your nose into the home inspection. You and your inspector will be looking at all sorts of things you might have skipped during your showings, like the attic and crawl space, and under the sinks. Don't be scared to delve into the details. Even the best home will receive a laundry list of to-do's and potential problems, and fixing them will be much easier with a hands-on understanding of the issues involved. Consider it free (and invaluable) fix-it advice.

Questions to ask a home inspector

What are some questions to ask a home inspector after he's finished the inspection? Because, let's face it, just staring at that hefty report highlighting every flaw in your future dream home can send many buyers into a full-blown panic!

Know the right questions to ask a home inspector afterward, though, and this can help put that report into perspective. Here are the big ones to hit.

"I don't understand [such and such], what does it mean?"

Just so you know what to expect, here's how it will go down: A day or two after the inspection, you should receive the inspector's report. It will be a detailed list of every flaw in the house, often along with pictures of some of the problem areas and more elaboration.

Hopefully, you also attended the actual inspection and could ask questions then; if so, the report should contain no surprises. It should contain what you talked about at the inspection, with pictures and perhaps a bit more detail. If there's anything major you don't remember from the inspection in the report, don't be afraid to ask about it.

"Is this a major or a minor problem?"

Keep in mind, most problems in the house will likely be minor and not outright deal breakers. Still, you'll want your home inspector to help you separate the two and point out any doozies. So ask him if there are any problems serious enough to keep you from moving forward with the house.

Keep in mind that ultimately, it's up to you and your real estate agent to determine how to address any issues.

"The inspector can't tell you, 'Make sure the seller pays for this,' so be sure you understand what needs to be done," says Lesh.

"Should I call in another expert for a follow-up inspection?"

Expect to have to call in other experts at this point, to look over major issues and assign a dollar figure to fixing them. If your inspector flags your electrical box as looking iffy, for example, you may need to have an electrician come take a look and tell you what exactly is wrong and what the cost would be to fix it. The same goes for any apparent problems with the heating or air conditioning, roof, or foundation. An HVAC repair person, roofer, or engineer will need to examine your house and provide a bid to repair the problem.

Why is this so important? This bid is what your real estate agent will take to the seller if you decide to ask for a concession instead of having the seller do the fix for you. Your inspector can't give you these figures, but he can probably give you a sense of whether it's necessary to call somebody in.

Home inspectors can advise you on whether to buy the house

"That's not my field of expertise," says Lesh. "Often people ask, 'Would you buy this house?' I can only tell you about the functioning portions of the house, not whether you should buy it." And don't forget: Even though most inspections are done at the buyer's request, inspectors are impartial. If you think inspections are meant to help the buyer renegotiate the purchase price, think again.

"Is there anything I'll need to do once I move in?"

Wait, you're still not done! It's easy to forget the inspector's report in the whirlwind of closing and moving, but there are almost always suggestions for things that need doing in the first two to three months of occupancy.

Lesh says he sometimes gets panicked calls from homeowners whose houses he has inspected three months after they've moved in. Although he's noted certain issues in his report, the buyers have neglected the report entirely—and paid for it later.

"I had a couple call and tell me they had seepage in the basement," Lesh says. "I pulled up their report and asked if they'd reconnected the downspout extension like I recommended. Nope. Well, there's your problem!"

Everything you didn't ask the seller to fix? That's your to-do list. Isn't owning a home fun?

Just remember—the vast majority of issues raised during a home inspection are repairable. Just as with a used car or an old computer, or second-hand clothing, there are bound to be problems. Some of them may be small and easily fixed, like leaky pipes and rattling doorknobs. But if an inspector discovers a *major* problem—with, say, the foundation or water intrusion—even that may not be a deal killer. In fact, it could be a bargaining chip you can discuss with the sellers before closing the deal.

Work with your real estate agent to determine the best approach. If your offer was contingent on a successful inspection (and most are), you have a good basis to request that the current owners make repairs before closing. You'll want to get this in writing, along with provisions to cover you if the sellers fail to fix the problems.

But there's no obligation for sellers to address the inspector's discoveries. If they aren't willing to shoulder the burden, you need to assess whether the cost of a new roof—or mold abatement, or fixing the foundation, or whatever the problem is—is worth the reward. With no solution beyond paying $30,000 out of your own pocket, you might need to move on to a more habitable home.

"People get very invested in the home they want to buy, and it all becomes a very overwhelmingly emotional experience," Singer says. "But they need to listen to the advice of the inspector, take a look at the financial ramifications, and make a clear-headed decision."

Chapter 12

The Home Closing: What to Expect

"ABC. A, always. B, be. C, closing. ALWAYS BE CLOSING. Always be closing."

—Alec Baldwin, *Glengarry Glen Ross*

The hardest parts are over: You've found that perfect home in a haystack of listings, negotiated a deal you're happy with, and secured a mortgage—and you're now in the home stretch of the home-buying process. Just one more critical hurdle lies ahead: the home closing. Also known as "settlement" or "escrow," this is a day when all involved parties meet to make this transaction official.

To make sure you're fully prepared, here's what to expect from the closing process, step by step—plus a handy checklist to keep it all straight.

☑ Get all contingencies squared away

Most purchase agreements have contingencies—things that buyers must do before this transaction is official, explains Jimmy Branham, a real estate agent at the Keyes Company, in Fort Lauderdale, FL. These are the most common contingencies you may have:

- Financing contingency

- Appraisal contingency

- Home inspection contingency

☑ Clear the title

When you buy a home, you "take title" to the property and establish legal ownership—a process that's confirmed by local public land records. As part of the closing process, your mortgage lender will require a title search, and you'll need to purchase title insurance to protect you from legal claims to the house.

Sometimes distant relatives—or an ex-spouse—may surface with a claim that they actually own the home, and that the seller had no right to sell it to you in the first place. But clearing title will ensure this doesn't happen, says Marc Israel, president and chief counsel of MiT National Land Services, a title company in New York City.

As the home buyer, you're entitled to choose the title company. You can get recommendations from your real estate agent, mortgage lender, and friends—just be sure to check out the license and reputation of each company online.

☑ Get final mortgage approval

Before you can go to the closing table, your home loan must go through the underwriting process. Underwriters are like real estate detectives—it's their job to make sure you have represented yourself and your finances truthfully, and that you haven't made any false or misleading claims on your loan application.

The underwriter—employed by your mortgage lender—will check your credit score, review your home appraisal, and ensure your financial portfolio has not changed since you were pre-approved for the loan.

Since underwriting typically happens shortly before closing, you don't want to do anything while you're in contract that's going to hurt your credit score. That includes buying a car, boat, or any other large purchase that has to be financed.

☑ Review your closing disclosure

If you're getting a loan, one of the best ways to prepare is to thoroughly review your closing disclosure. This official document outlines your exact mortgage payments, the loan's terms (e.g., the interest rate and duration), and additional fees you'll pay, called closing costs.

You'll want to compare your closing disclosure to the loan estimate your lender gave you at the outset. If you spot any discrepancies, ask your lender to explain them.

☑ Do a final walk-through

Most sales contracts allow buyers to do a walk-through of the home within 24 hours before closing. During this stage, you're making sure the previous owner has vacated (unless you've allowed a rent-back arrangement in which they can stick around for a period of time before moving). You're also double-checking that the home is in the condition agreed upon in the contract. If your home inspection revealed problems that the sellers had agreed to fix, you'll want to make sure those repairs were made.

☑ Bring the necessary documentation to closing

Make sure you have the following items when you head to the closing table:

- Proof of homeowners insurance

- A copy of your contract with the seller

- Your home inspection reports

- Any paperwork your lender required to approve your loan

- A government-issued photo ID. (Note to newlyweds who just changed their name: The ID needs to match the name that will appear on the property's title and mortgage.)

Once closing day has arrived, here's what to expect:

A bunch of people: Exactly who will be present at a closing (and where it's held) depends on the state you live in, but there are certain supporting characters you can usually expect to make an appearance. The cast includes the home seller, the seller's real estate agent as well as your own, buyer and seller attorneys, a representative from a title company (more on that below), and, occasionally, a representative from the bank or lender that is underwriting your loan.

Signing your name a lot: You'll be putting your John Hancock on a pile of legal documents (so be prepared for a mild hand cramp if you're not used to writing in cursive).

A few curveballs: Be prepared for things to go awry at the closing, for example, someone gets stuck in traffic, a document is missing, or a name is misspelled. But don't stress; simply do what's in your power to make the day go off without a hitch. For instance, don't schedule something two hours after the closing is supposed to start, in case your closing runs over.

Plus: Watch out! 5 things never to say at the closing table

By the time home buyers make it to the closing, it's smooth sailing, right? *Wrong.*

For home buyers, the adage "Loose lips sink ships" is pretty darn spot on as a best strategy at settlement. In fact, "There are things that home buyers could say that could stop the closing *entirely*," warns Jennifer Baxter, associate broker at Re/Max Regency in Suwanee, GA.

Granted, many states do not have closings where you must show up in person. Still, if you live in an area where that's still required or customary, you'll definitely want to do all you can to raise the odds that all goes smoothly. To help, here are five things you should never, ever say at closing.

"I quit my job this morning"

Before a mortgage lender approves your loan, the company's underwriter will do a final review to verify that your employment status hasn't changed since you were pre-approved for the mortgage. That usually takes place a couple of days before closing, so if you just quit (or got fired), your lender might be caught by surprise. Surprise is not good. In fact, you might need to sign a document at closing confirming that your employment status has not changed.

"I can't wait to get all the new furniture we bought"

Before approving the loan, your mortgage lender will also check to make sure your credit score remains unchanged before closing. If your score *has* changed, the company might raise your loan's interest rate, says Judy Weiniger, broker associate and CEO at Weiniger Group in Warren, NJ.

So what does this have to do with furniture? Using a credit card to buy furniture—or getting a loan to buy a car—could negatively affect your credit score. And, sadly, credit-damaging behavior is a common mistake.

A recent TransUnion study found that consumers increase their credit card spending as much as two or three times their previous rate just before they close on a home.

The lesson? At closing, it's best to avoid talking about anything that could have potentially affected your credit score, in case your lender uses this info against you.

"I can't believe the appraisal came in $20,000 above the sales price"

A home appraisal, you might recall, is where a lender assesses how much the home is worth. This price might be different from what *you're* paying for the place. If the appraised value is higher, that means you got a bargain. Congrats!

Go ahead and high-five yourself all you want; however, don't share this news with the home seller, since it means he clearly *didn't* luck out in this transaction, and sold his home for less than what it might really be worth. As the home buyer, you aren't required to share with the seller what the home appraised for. Thus, Baxter advises home buyers to keep that information private.

"If you're getting a great deal, there's no need to rub it in the seller's face," Baxter says.

"I can't wait to gut the house"

If you're planning to remodel the property, just don't mention that in front of the seller, says Weiniger. "Many home sellers still have an emotional attachment to their house," she says. "They don't want to hear that you're going to walk in and just start tearing down walls."

"Could you remove that swing set from the backyard?"

Closing is neither the time nor place to make last-minute requests of the seller. The exception would be if there's an issue related to home inspection repairs that you found during the final walk-through, in which case you should *absolutely* speak up, says Weiniger.

However, if you failed to make your offer contingent on anything, it's your responsibility to take care of it—not the seller's.

If all goes well, as it usually does, you will eventually leave your home closing with a stack of documents (which you should save) and, last, but definitely not least, the keys to your new home.

Chapter 13

Tips, Hacks, and Tricks to Master Your Move

> "It is a comfortable feeling to know that you stand on your own ground. Land is about the only thing that can't fly away."
>
> —Anthony Trollope, *The Last Chronicles of Barset*

Finally.

You've slapped your John Hancock on the closing paperwork. You're happy with your loan ... well, as happy as you can be, considering the magnitude of the debt you just accepted. Stress dreams have mostly subsided, barring the occasional vision of some movers dropping your grandmother's curio cabinet, shattering this priceless antique while they run off with your money.

Moving can be a pain in the you-know-what. That's why we'll share some expert tips and tricks to make the process as easy and pain-free as possible.

POP QUIZ

Just how stressful is moving?

According to a recent survey by energy company E.ON, moving is so tough, it actually tops the list of life's most stressful moments, beating out divorce and starting a new job!

How to get a moving estimate that won't become a moving target

Moving can get even *more* stressful when you don't know how to get a moving estimate you can trust. This can lead to massive misunderstandings, when movers quote you one price before you move, and a different (and much higher!) number after it's over.

So what gives?

The fact is, there are many ways to get a moving estimate, and they all come with their pros and cons. Here's what you need to know to get an estimate you can trust.

How a moving cost calculator can help

For starters, you can get an instant estimate for your move using a moving cost calculator, which will ballpark the cost of your move based on the number of rooms you have, how far you're moving, and other variables.

Just keep in mind that a moving calculator is just a ballpark start. To get a more accurate estimate, you'll have to actually contact a moving company and get its take on the situation.

POP QUIZ

How much will moving cost?

According to the American Moving and Storage Association (AMSA), the average cost of an in-state move is $2,300. That's for four movers at $200 per hour, based on an average weight of 7,400 pounds. The average cost of an out-of-state move averaging 1,225 miles is $4,300.

Binding vs. nonbinding estimate: What's the difference?

So you want to know precisely how much your move is going to cost? Get a binding estimate, where a moving company tells you upfront all of your moving costs, including fees, taxes, and insurance. According to the Federal Motor Carrier Safety Administration (FMCSA), movers who provide a binding estimate can't require consumers to pay any more than the estimated amount at delivery.

There are a couple of caveats, though. Getting a binding estimate upfront may incur an initial fee. And with a binding estimate, "Movers will often charge more money to build in an extra cushion, in case the move takes longer than expected," says Scott Michael, AMSA's president and CEO.

By comparison, a nonbinding estimate is free, but the cost that you're quoted is only an estimate, and is subject to change. If the nonbinding estimate is based on weight, the movers can charge up to 10% more once they get the official weight on your goods, after packing them into the vehicle and stopping at a weigh station.

How far do people move?

Not very! According to NAR, home buyers typically only move about 15 miles from where they lived previously.

Get your moving estimate in person

You can obtain a moving estimate over the phone, by email, or in person. Michael recommends getting estimates from at least three movers in person.

"Doing it in person ensures that the mover will see all the items that need to be shipped, and can identify any complications in advance," Michael says. "For instance, if there are low-hanging tree branches that would prevent the moving truck from being able to pull up to your house, that's something you want to know ahead of time."

To obtain an accurate estimate, you'll want to do a walk-through of your home with the mover a couple of weeks before your move. Michael recommends going room to room with the mover, "showing the person every single item the company is going to move."

Point out items that you plan to transport yourself, and flag valuables, like artwork or antiques, that need to be handled differently or insured at a higher rate. "You may need to get an insurance policy from a third party to cover extraordinary artwork," Michael says.

How to find reputable movers

To find a reputable moving company, make sure it has a state license to operate—and it should be happy to show you proof.

If you're moving out of state, you'll need a mover that also has a unique license number, issued by the United States Department of Transportation.

Unfortunately, every year, thousands of people fall victim to moving fraud, according to the FMCSA's "Protect Your Move" campaign. To avoid getting scammed, steer clear of moving companies that ask for a deposit, list a P.O. Box or a residential address, or offer a ridiculously lowball estimate.

The ultimate moving checklist

With all the excitement of new digs, it's easy to forget some important tasks. So, before you move, check out this moving checklist to know what should be done long before you settle in.

☑ Turn on utilities

Electric, gas, water—don't assume they'll be on and operational when you arrive. Instead, get all your utilities set up ahead of time.

"Chances are the seller will be turning them off as of the closing date," says Greg Beckman, an Annapolis, MD, real estate agent.

☑ Set up internet and cable service

Plan on having a "Property Brothers" marathon while you're unpacking? Have your home wired for service before you arrive, advises Julie McDonough, a real estate agent in Southern California.

☑ Order an energy audit

One of the best ways to cut your energy bill is to order a home energy audit, says Rachel Foy, a real estate agent in Newton, MA.

An energy audit is a professional assessment of your new home's overall energy performance. This will show you how to make your house more energy-efficient (think insulating the attic, weather-stripping windows, sealing air leaks in crawl spaces), so it's best to have one done and to make any related repairs before moving in.

A home energy audit costs, on average, about $215 to $600, but some utility companies will do them for free.

☑ Do a deep clean

Break out the heavy-duty cleaning supplies! Because after all, "It's never easier to do a deep clean than when the house is empty," Beckman says.

☑ Change the locks

This is a basic safety measure; however, "It can't be done until after closing," says Chris Dossman, a real estate agent in Indianapolis.

☑ Don't forget the utilities

You don't want a sudden power outage one month after your move—let alone an outage that is your own darn fault.

"Many sellers are focused on their new move, and sometimes utilities are forgotten in the mix," says Fox. By the time you move in, you should get in touch with all of your new providers to switch services into your name. If you're moving into a standalone house from an apartment, you might be surprised by the variety of utilities you need to set up.

Long before your move, try to check with the former owners to determine specifically what you're paying for and what you need to set up, but expect to pay for water, gas, electricity, and trash—as well as any cable TV or Internet services you desire.

☑ Test smoke and carbon monoxide detectors

Make sure these are functioning properly to protect your new home from fires and other emergencies.

☑ Set up the alarm system

If the home already has a security system installed, call the provider to confirm that service is set up, says Jennifer Baxter, associate broker at Re/Max Regency in Suwanee, GA.

☑ Forward your mail

Don't forget to update your address with the United States Postal Service. (Visit the Official Postal Service Change of Address website.) The postal service charges a $1 fee to verify your identity when changing your address online, so you'll need a credit or debit card.

Note: The postal service will stop forwarding periodicals to your new address 60 days after you move, so alert magazines and newspapers to the fact that you've moved.

☑ Update your billing address

Inform your credit card companies, banks, or any other financial institutions, about your new address. Also, if you frequently buy anything from a website, you can avoid future headaches by updating your profile with your new address.

☑ Change the locks

As soon as you get the chance, hire a locksmith to change all the locks on your house (don't forget the back entrance or any other access points). While we're certain the seller is trustworthy, you never know who else might have keys to your new home. Better to be safe than sorry.

Doors aren't the only locks that need changing: Buyers who use a community mailbox should make sure to have it rekeyed by the local post office, which should cost about $40 or $50. That's not much at all for peace of mind that no one is digging through your mail.

☑ Check in with the homeowners association (HOA)

Does your new home have a homeowners association? If so, contact the HOA to make sure everything is up to date. You're likely to need to fill out transfer paperwork so it has a record of the new ownership. Even great HOAs can be difficult to deal with, requiring meticulous paperwork and cumbersome restrictions, so make sure you understand the bylaws and neighborhood restrictions of your HOA. You don't want to get off on the wrong foot with your new neighbors, so full knowledge of how the association works is absolutely necessary.

☑ Make a detailed list of your belongings

Moving is a complicated, messy affair—so take the opportunity to make an inventory of your belongings during packing, labeling each box with what's in it.

"You'll be grateful for the detailed description of contents stored within the myriad packing boxes that now surround you," says Fox. There's a bonus: A home inventory is worth its weight in gold if you have any sort of accident, such as a fire, or if a natural disaster leaves your home a wreck.

☑ Buy fire extinguishers

Get one for every level of your home, make sure you know how to use it, and plan an escape route in the event of a fire.

☑ Childproof the home

Have kids? Every year, millions of children are hospitalized because of accidents around the home, according to Safe Kids Worldwide. So, before your bundle of joy starts toddling around the house, take steps to fully childproof your new home.

☑ Figure out the best nearby takeout

All done? Boxes in place, furniture in your house—if not in the right spot? Movers gone? The proper way to celebrate is with takeout and beer, eaten on the floor. Do your research ahead of time, so you know what you want to eat, and aren't left scrambling an hour before closing time.

"Know where the best pizza place or takeout is nearby," says Eileen O'Reilly, a real estate agent in Burlingame, CA. "When you are crazy busy with moving in, you don't want to get hangry."

Congratulations! You're finished ... until it's time to sell, that is.

In the meantime, though, it's time to resume doing what this whole journey is all about: enjoying your amazing new digs.

After moving into a home, how long will you stay?

According to NAR, buyers expect to hunker down in their homes for about 15 years, and 19% say they plan never to move again!

Glossary

Active listing

An "active" real estate listing status means that a property is currently on the market and available for sale. It may have received offers, but none have yet been accepted, which means that the opportunity is wide open for other buyers to make a proposal.

Active with contract (AWC)

This real estate listing status means that even though there's an accepted offer on the home, the seller is looking for backup offers in case the primary buyer falls through. While any seller can entertain backup offers as a precautionary measure, as long as this is made clear in the contract, this term most often crops up with short sales, since they can often fall through, and it can be helpful if a second buyer is waiting in the wings.

Adjustable-Rate Mortgage (ARM)

This type of mortgage does exactly what it says: Its interest rate will be adjusted by the lender in accordance with current interest rates, after an introductory period that could be three, five, seven, or 10 years. The good news? The initial ARM interest rate is usually lower than that of a fixed-rate mortgage. The bad news? If interest rates go up, so do your interest rate and payments, once the introductory period is over.

ARM caps

If you want an adjustable-rate mortgage but want to avoid the heart attack that comes with skyrocketing interest rates, you'll need an ARM cap. The cap limits how high the bank can nudge up the interest rate on your loan, thus limiting your monthly payments (and blood pressure). You may pay a bit more for this privilege.

Back on market (BOM)

This is a property that has come back on the market after a pending sale. This means that the home fell out of escrow, perhaps due to contract issues.

Closed listing (CL)

This real estate listing status means the property is sold and no longer available.

Closing

Also known as settlement, the closing is the final stretch of your real estate transaction, which involves bringing together lawyers, real estate agents, buyers, and sellers at the closing table. At the closing, the buyer will provide the funds to purchase the home. It's also when you get the keys to your new home.

Closing costs

When home buyers arrive at the closing—the day they sign all the paperwork and receive the keys—they are responsible for paying closing costs. Those are the various fees for the services and processing necessary to make a mortgage happen. So, bring your checkbook and a decent pen! You shouldn't be blindsided by the amount of the closing costs, because within three days of receiving your loan application, the lender must provide you with a three-page "loan estimate" that lays out the various fees.

Comparative Market Analysis (CMA)

Short for comparative market analysis or competitive market analysis, a CMA is a report showing "comps," which detail the location, size, and recent sales price of homes in a certain area. Home sellers (and their real estate agents) use CMAs to help them come up with their asking price, while buyers can use CMAs to come up with how much to offer on a particular home.

Comps

Short for housing "comparables," comps are homes similar to the one you're hoping to buy, in terms of location, size, number of bedrooms/bathrooms, style, amenities, and (last but not least) sales price. Comps are used to create a comparative market analysis (CMA).

Condo

A condo, short for "condominium," is a private residence owned by an individual or family in a building or community with multiple units. Although condos are usually part of a larger building, "detached condominiums" also exist. What *all* condos have in common is that they share with other units common areas—such as yards, garages, rec rooms, or gyms—that the condo owners don't have to maintain themselves, making home upkeep that much easier.

Contingencies

Contingencies are requirements that must be met before a real estate deal can close. The specific contingencies are set and agreed upon by the buyer and seller. The customary ones for the buyer's loan are a property appraisal, financing, and home inspection. All contingencies must be resolved before a sale is final.

Deal pending (DP)

This real estate listing status means that the seller has an accepted offer on the house and an executed contract, and that all the contingencies have been met, so the home is pending sale. Even though a sale is highly likely, some pending properties may still accept backup offers.

Disclosures

All sellers are required to fill out a property disclosure for buyers that states everything they know about the home since they've owned it, whether it's good (there's a brand-new roof) or bad (the basement leaks during heavy rains). A seller who intentionally withholds information is committing fraud, so when in doubt, it's best to 'fess up!

Down payment

This is the money home buyers must pay upfront when purchasing a home. Generally, a down payment totaling 20% of the price of the house is ideal (so, for example, expect to put a $50,000 down payment on a $250,000 house), since this allows you to avoid paying a monthly fee called private mortgage insurance (PMI). However, certain buyers can purchase a home with as little as 3.5% down with an FHA loan, or 0% down with a VA loan.

Due diligence

Due diligence is a fancy term for "Do your homework." Before buying a property, you should fully investigate it for potential problems that could cost major money to fix after you've moved in. If the buyers discover negative information regarding the property during this time, they can cancel the purchase.

Duplex

A duplex is not just one home, but two. They may be stacked one on top of the other on separate floors, or they may be side by side, with a shared wall. A duplex may also be called a "multifamily dwelling," because more than one family can live in it.

Earnest money

Also known as "good-faith money," earnest money is a sum put up by the buyer and generally held in escrow or trust to show the buyer is serious about purchasing the home. There is no defined amount, but earnest money generally runs about 1% to 2% of the purchase price. When the purchase is complete, that money is applied toward closing costs. If the contract doesn't go through, there are guidelines that vary by state, which determine which party will be awarded the escrow deposit.

Effective date

The date that the last party signed or initialed any terms and/or changes in the sales contract. This is often the date that starts the clock on the contract's various deadlines (for example, that a home inspection must happen within 10 days).

Escrow

In the home-buying process, escrow is a secure holding area where important items (like the earnest money check and contracts) are kept safe until the deal is closed and the house officially changes hands. The escrow officer is a third party—perhaps someone from the closing company, an attorney, or a title company agent (customs vary by state). The third party is there to make sure everything during the closing proceeds smoothly, including the transfers of money and documents. Escrow protects all the relevant parties by ensuring that no funds and property change hands until all conditions in the agreement have been met.

Expired listing

This means that the property listing has expired and is no longer active, usually because it didn't sell. That could mean the seller is still open to accepting an offer, so it's worth touching base if your curiosity is piqued.

Federal Housing Administration (FHA) loan

This is a loan backed by the Federal Housing Administration—ideal for first-time home buyers, since the down payment can be as low as 3.5%. Buyers are also required to pay mortgage insurance—either upfront or over the life of the loan—which hovers at around 1% of the cost of your loan.

Fixed-rate mortgage

With this type of mortgage, once you lock in your interest rate with your lender, that's it: The rate remains fixed—your monthly payments will remain the same for the life of the mortgage. This can be good or bad, but it will always be *predictable*. While shopping around for the lowest rate, you will notice that interest on fixed-rate mortgages is almost always higher initially than on adjustable-rate mortgages (ARMs). But over the long run, avoiding the uncertainty of sudden rate hikes might be worth the peace of mind.

Foreclosure

A foreclosure happens when a homeowner doesn't pay his or her mortgage for an extended period, so the bank or entity that lent that money takes possession of the home—which means the current owner must move out.

For Sale by Owner (FSBO)

FSBO (pronounced "fizbo") stands for "for sale by owner," which means that the homeowners haven't retained a real estate agent to help them sell their house.

Full bath

In order for a room to be listed as a "full bath," it must contain four key fixtures: a toilet, sink, bathtub, and shower (or shower/bath combo).

Half bath

A half-bath, also known as a powder room or guest bath, typically has only a toilet and sink. A three-quarter bathroom (yes, that's a thing, too) most often has an upright stall shower, a sink, and a toilet. But in older houses or condos, a three-quarter bath might have just a sink, toilet, and tub, but no shower.

Homeowners association (HOA)

If you're buying a condo, townhouse, or freestanding home in a neighborhood with shared common areas—such as a swimming pool, parking garage, or even just the security gates and sidewalks in front of each residence—odds are these areas are maintained by a homeowners association, or HOA. HOAs help ensure that your community looks its best and functions smoothly. And the number of Americans living in HOAs is on the rise, growing from a mere 1% in 1970 to 1 in 4 today.

Home appraisal

If a buyer is getting a mortgage, the lender requires the buyer to pay for a home appraisal. That's where a third party comes in and estimates the value of the house, making sure a lender's money isn't going toward a lemon. (If a buyer is paying all cash, an appraisal is optional.)

Home inspection

Before purchasing a home, buyers are often strongly encouraged to get a home inspection—where a professional home inspector visits the house and checks it for potential problems that might make it dangerous to live there, or be expensive to fix. Depending on what issues are found, the buyer can:

- Accept the property in the current condition and move forward.

- Release the contract and retain the earnest money.

- Ask the seller to repair issues discovered during the inspection.

Multiple Listing Service (MLS)

The multiple listing service is a massive database of homes for sale, searchable by price, neighborhood, and home features. While home buyers can't view the MLS in full (only real estate agents can do that), you can access highly condensed versions of MLS listings on various online sites like realtor.com.

Pending, showing for backup

This real estate listing status means that the property's owners are actively taking backup offers in case the first one falls through.

Pending, subject to lender approval

This listing status means the seller has an accepted offer, but is waiting to see if the buyer's bank will agree to it. If not, it could end up back on the market, so go ahead and inquire if you're interested.

Pocket listing

Sometimes high-profile sellers (like celebrities) will choose not to list their home on the MLS, for privacy reasons, such as to avoid publicity. A property that is not entered into the MLS is often called a pocket listing, since it's "hidden in an agent's pocket." That means that only those potential buyers with whom an agent works directly will be aware that the home is on the market.

Points

Points are part of closing costs charged by your mortgage lender. There are two types of mortgage points.

- **Origination points**: These points are charged to recover some costs of the loan origination process. This would include compensating your loan officer, notary fees, preparation costs, and inspection fees.

- **Discount points**: These points, also known as positive points, lower your interest rate but increase your closing costs, because payment for them is due at closing. They are a kind of prepaid interest you "buy" from your lender for a lower interest rate.

So how much will points cost you? One "point" equals 1% of your loan (or $3,000 on a $300,000 mortgage), two points equal 2% ($6,000), etc.

Principal

After you've made your down payment on a house, the rest of the money you still owe your lender is called the principal. This mortgage term refers to what you will be paying off, monthly, over the lifetime of the mortgage, which can last anywhere from five to 30 years—usually 30.

Seller's market

A seller's market is one where there are more home buyers than sellers. Based on basic laws of supply and demand, this means sellers have the upper hand: They will likely sell their place quickly, perhaps for over asking price, with a minimum of fuss or pushback from buyers. Meanwhile, home buyers in seller's markets face a tough road: Due to increased competition, they'll have to act fast, bid high, and generally bend over backwards to woo sellers into accepting their offer over the many that may be at their disposal.

Short sale

This is a situation where you're selling your home, and the offer you get is so low that it won't cover the total amount you owe on your mortgage. However, because you need to unload your house, you'll take it. This is a short sale—simply put, you end up "short" on paying back your lender, and the bank agrees to accept less than what's owed on the loan. Often homeowners are pushed into a short sale by personal financial troubles that make it impossible to pay their monthly mortgage. At the same time, they find it hard to sell at a price that would enable them to pay off their loan—especially if local real estate market trends have driven down their home's value. Short sales happened in many communities across the nation during the housing bust of the mid-late 2000s.

Temporarily off the market (TOM)

This means the homeowner has removed the property from the MLS for an undetermined period, usually because work is being done on the house or because the home cannot be shown. It should return to active soon enough, so it's certainly worth piping up if you're smitten.

Title search

A title search or survey basically confirms that the property is owned fair and square by the seller, who can then transfer those rights to the buyer. Occasionally, a home's title can be compromised by long-lost heirs or liens by contractors who did work on the property but never got paid. The good news is that you can buy title insurance in case long-buried issues crop up down the road.

Townhouse

These are single-family dwellings with at least two floors that share a wall with another house. Townhouses are common in densely populated urban areas, and are often an affordable option for people who can't afford (or don't want the hassles of) a free-standing house.

Under contract (UC)

This real estate listing status means the seller has an agreed-upon contract with the potential buyer. That doesn't mean that it's a done deal by any means, however, since the contract may contain contingencies that must be met before the home sale goes through.

U.S. Department of Agriculture (USDA) loan

USDA Rural Development loans are designed for families in rural areas. The government finances 100% of the home price—in other words, no down payment necessary—and offers discounted interest rates to boot. The catch? Your debt load cannot exceed your income by more than 41%, and you will be required to purchase mortgage insurance.

Veterans Affairs (VA) loan

If you've served in the United States military, a Veterans Affairs loan can be an excellent alternative to a traditional mortgage. If you qualify, you can score a sweet home with no money down and no mortgage insurance requirements.

Withdrawn listing

This means the property was withdrawn from the realty market. This might be for a variety of reasons: The sellers may have decided they want to stay put, or they may just not have received any offers they liked. Take-home lesson for buyers? If you adore what you see in the listing, it certainly can't hurt to inquire.

Additional Resources

To buy a home:

realtor.com

To sell a home:

realtor.com/sell

To find a real estate agent or broker:

realtor.com/realestateagents

To find a mortgage:

realtor.com/mortgage

To learn more about buying your first home:

realtor.com/welcome/first-time-buyer

To calculate what price home you can afford:

realtor.com/mortgage/tools/affordability-calculator

To figure out if it's cheaper to buy or rent in your area:

realtor.com/mortgage/tools/rent-or-buy-calculator